Best Wishes!
Alma L. Carr-Jones
10-1-21

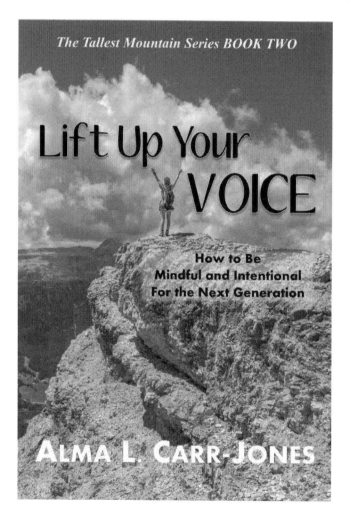

The Tallest Mountain Series BOOK TWO

Lift Up Your VOICE

How to Be Mindful and Intentional For the Next Generation

ALMA L. CARR-JONES

Paperback ISBN-13: 978-1-948026-66-6
Digital ISBN-13: 978-1-948026-79-6

Unless otherwise noted, Scriptures are taken from the Holy Bible, New International Version®, NIV®. Copyright © 1973, 1978, 1984, 2011 by Biblica, Inc.™ Used by permission of Zondervan. All rights reserved worldwide. www.zondervan.com.

Scripture quotations marked "KJV" are from the King James Version by public domain.

Scripture quotations marked "NKJV" are taken from The New King James Version / Thomas Nelson Publishers, Nashville: Thomas Nelson Publishers., Copyright © 1982. Used by permission. All rights reserved.

Scripture quotations marked "NASB" are taken from the New American Standard Bible®, Copyright © 1960, 1971, 1977, 1995, 2020 by The Lockman Foundation. All rights reserved.

Scripture quotations market "NET" are taken from the NET Bible® copyright ©1996-2017 by Biblical Studies Press, L.L.C. http://netbible.com All rights reserved.

Scripture quotations marked "CEV" are taken from the Contemporary English Version (CEV) Copyright © 1995 by American Bible Society.

Scripture quotations marked "ESV" are taken from The Holy Bible, English Standard Version. ESV® Text Edition: 2016. Copyright © 2001 by Crossway Bibles, a publishing ministry of Good News Publishers.

Published by TMP Books, 3 Central Plaza Ste 307, Rome, GA 30161

www.TMPBooks.com

In Memoriam

This poem is written for my "baby from another lady" in memory
of her daughter, Alisha (Keshia).

Geraldine, you already know that I love you so much
You have that special something about you
-A sweetness that shows GOD's loving touch.

To know you is to know
That there are angels that walk among us
Like stars that shine so bright
Sunny dispositions full of love for us all
Gladdening our days and shortening our nights
Geraldine and Keshia, mother and daughter
Kindred spirits whose life and legacy
Strengthen us day by day
Because to have known her
And to know you leaves a warmth
That lingers and will do so
Even when our paths no longer cross
And each of us has gone our separate way!

Dedicated to

YHWH, The HEAD of my life.

YOU brought us through the pandemic

And so much more

I just want to thank YOU, SIR

My gratitude and love to YOU

The MAKER of this and the other shore.

Also Dedicated to

My Momma, Lula Mae Peters Carr (R.I.P.)

Brendell Cowan for her sunny disposition and encouragement.

Faye Cross for her unwavering friendship, support, push, and lofty vision.

Sylvia Nance for her true friendship and heart.

My Publisher, Tracy Ruckman, for her belief in me.

My cousins, Bertha, Douglas, Essie, Lula, Linda.

Acknowledgements and Thanks

I want to extend grateful thanks to all the readers of my books and especially to the congregations that have chosen to use my books in their Ladies' classes.

May they be a blessing to you as we all wrap our arms around the church of tomorrow, backpacks and all.

My *Love for God and His love for me is not my best*
Kept secret as a Christian because He gave His
Love to me for me to give it away
And to keep giving and giving even
After my body has gone back to the clay.

Table of Contents

Introduction

Lift Up Your Voice is a continuation of ***Get Yourself Up*** and is Book Two in *The Tallest Mountain Series* and focuses on being mindful and intentional for the next generation. It further teaches us how to keep our faith intact when we are thrown way out of our comfort zones. With the advent and progression of COVID-19 all of us felt that way in that it felt like the bottom of our world was falling out and nothing made sense anymore, from toilet paper shortages to hundreds of thousands of deaths and the way we, as a world, dealt with all of it.

But I must admit, even before the advent of the coronavirus (Covid-19), each successive generation of Americans seems to be getting further away from GOD, because each generation reports a lower percentage of Christians, according to a Pew Study. "Older generations of Americans are not passing along the Christian faith as effectively as their forebears."[1] Some people do not even want HIS NAME called.

So, when the coronavirus or COVID-19 began to change lifestyles and economic statuses in a big way, I thought about 2 Chronicles 7:14, which reads:

> "If my people who are called by my name will humble themselves and pray and seek my face, and turn from

---

[1] https://www.cnn.com/2015/05/12/living/pew-religion-study/index.html

their wicked ways; then I will hear from heaven, will forgive their sin, and will heal their land."

The Bible says in Psalm 30:5,

> For HIS anger is but for a moment,
> HIS favor is for a lifetime;
> Weeping may last for the night,
> But a shout of joy comes in the morning.

And I further thought about Deuteronomy 4:31, which says that GOD is a compassionate GOD. And I remember what I read in Hebrews, Chapter 6, verse 10:

> "God is not unjust; He will not forget your work and the love you have shown Him as you have helped His people and continue to help them."

So what this says to me is that if you are HIS faithful working child, HE sees and knows your work and will not forget all that you do in His name for love of HIM and for love of your fellow man.

That verse further tells me to stop worrying about whether I, along with the rest of the Christians in America and the world, have been abandoned by the LORD.

That verse lets me know that HE sees my worries and knows my heart, and that He will not abandon us.

Those scriptures buoyed up my soul so much, I decided to share that buoyancy with my fellow man using the God-given talent that I have.

Lift Up Your Voice

Are you a little weary soul, tired in these COVID-19 faith-trying times? Just know that GOD loves us all and as long as we give our heart to HIM, remain faithful to HIM, HE will bring us through.

Let us always remember that we are in the spotlight as Christians and that we train by example as well as well as with words. Remember that our voice needs to be heard, and understood, by the next generation. Now is the time to lift up YOUR voice and be heard.

I will talk a bit more about the pandemic and how it has affected us in my latest standalone book, ***Renewal of Joy***, that will be released in conjunction with the final book in The Tallest Mountain Series, Book 3, ***Bear the Good News***.

Enjoy this book, as it is a labor of love from my heart to yours.

Lesson 5:

Sowing and Reaping

Scripture: Galatians 6:7; Ephesians 6:8; Matthew 6:14-15

Aim: TO BE MINDFUL OF THE FACT THAT all deeds come back to us multiplied. TO BE MINDFUL OF THE FACT THAT forgiveness is something we all need.

Song: You Will Reap What You Sow

One of three main problems that you have when trying to live the life of a Christian is negativity. There are just some people or haters that seem to thrive on negativity. They won't do anything and don't want you to, either. That is just a fact of life. Though it is troubling when said folk set their sights on you, keep your hand in God's hand and step on because negativity has its own reward (Galatians 6:7, KJV), as does positivity. (Ephesians 6:8, KJV)

You have heard all your life that, "The end justifies the means." Well, does it really? If you look throughout the annals of Biblical history, you will see that that saying is not *necessarily* so. I say not necessarily because so often, people will use the saying from sentence one above to justify wrongdoing for selfish gain. They adopt the motto of, "It's what I want and that is all that matters." But that is not necessarily pleasant. Pharaoh used *"any means necessary"* to get what he wanted or so he thought. But take a look at this. He was allowed to become ruler of Egypt because the Lord had a purpose in mind for him. He thought that he was getting what he wanted, and he was doing it by any means necessary, even thwarting God.

You Better Ask Somebody

- If he could speak today, Pharaoh would tell you from his watery grave that it does not pay to trifle with God's people. He thought that he was going to make God's people turn around and go back to Egypt, but God had other plans. You know the story, so I won't trouble you with the retelling of it here. (Read Exodus 14.)
- Nehemiah's enemies thought that they were going to get him to come down from the wall, but the Lord had other plans. (Nehemiah 6:3, KJV) Nehemiah told his oppressors that he could not stop the work that he was doing for God. He told them that he could not come down.

There are so many others that I could mention, but I won't for time's sake. But I will say this. If you are doing a good work for the Lord and you have trouble because of your work, don't despair. You keep going and you keep your faith in God. He sees your pain, anguish, and mistreatment. He sees the ditches dug for you, etc.

"Be still and know." And then step on in His name. He knows and cares. Remember Romans 8:31.

Yes, there are times in life that the wattage of your smile may have that wattage like a bulb just before it blows, but the smile is there. You and I both know that when you get to a quiet place at home you give vent to any pent-up hurts, frustrations, etc. when you talk to God. Then with your faith renewed, you get back in the fray for the next round. But you are better equipped now. You can even look at your enemies with a serene smile because you know Who laughs in heaven (Psalm 37:13 & Psalm 1:1-6) and Who walks with you.

Sometimes when your enemies think they have you cornered and are busy watching you to see if your pot will boil, God causes another pot to be put on and to boil at full steam.

Keep Going

Yes, in your walk for the Lord, some folk will look at you as weak and helpless. It is like the predator instinct kicks in and you look like easy picking. You appear to be helpless just about like a deer in headlights or a bunny tied to a stake as bait for a larger animal, but with a cage that drops down around the bunny before the animal that is hunting it can devour it. I don't know, maybe my example might not be as true as a real hunter would make it, but you get my drift. You, dear heart, keep going. God sees; He knows, and He cares about you, and He laughs!

Passing Forward/Forgiving

Love is the key to relationships in the world. If folk just remember what the Lord has said about love, they will remember that they are to treat others the way they themselves want to be treated. It is as simple as that.

A better life begins with the simple acts of apologizing and forgiving. If you practice apologizing and forgiving, you will be starting to use better building blocks in your relationships with your fellowman (sowing seeds). When you act with love toward your fellowman, more likely than not, he will pass a similar act on to someone that he meets, and then it becomes a chain of positive events. That is called sharing or spreading the love.

Whatever you do, make sure that you are not the one who causes someone to whisper brokenly to God, "That person hurt my feelings."

Good Seeds Grown

Did you know

That the seeds of kindness sown

Will yield a crop of blessings when grown?

When you do a kind deed it blesses the person you did it for and you, too. Both of you get the endorphin rush when you do the deed, but does the blessing from the kindness stop there? If this kind deed is done to a child, you might encourage a future doctor, lawyer, scientist, astronaut, disease researcher, world renown evangelist, etc. Or it might just be done to a person who will always be a regular ordinary soul. Then too, it could be that a visitor from another realm has been sent to see how you would react. (… entertained angels unawares, Hebrews 13:2, KJV)

One kind deed is like a seed planted and the more seeds you plant the greater your harvest, even if some seed does fall on stony or rocky ground. Picture, if you will, a pea harvesting season. Every pod of peas on the vine came from one seed. And, as I am sure you have heard, some peas can be dried and preserved for next year's planting and others frozen or canned for food for the winter season and still others cooked and shared with the local homeless shelter not even counting what you cook up for your family. All that bounty came from one pea!

Now

You know how tired you get when bushel after bushel of peas have to be shelled? Sometimes you find yourself wondering when you will get finished. Imagine if all those peas were blessings poured upon you! You would be rolling over in contentment and joy, and goodwill, wouldn't you? Yes, you would!

My Point

No matter how you are ridiculed for performing acts of kindness, keep going, dear. There's a blessing in your sowing, a blessing for you, your family and countless others. How many times will that seed reproduce and send you another harvest?

How Many Times

Kindness has not gone out of style and let's keep it so

For you never know when the seeds that you have planted

Carried by the winds of reaping, will crop

Up on a row that you have to hoe

My, my, my, what a bountiful blessing, a good seed to sow!

What a Blessing!

How many peas in a pod

How many pods on a vine

From just one single pea I see

The bountiful blessing from just being kind

And lending a helping hand in loving generosity.

As Easy as Saying, "Thank You."

Such a simple phrase, yet it conveys a great sentiment, and we use it quite a bit. We have no problem using it because it is the "right thing to do." By the same token, we should have no problem using the words, "Forgive me, or I forgive." Afterall, it is the right thing to do. You know how much we need and depend upon the Lord's forgiveness of us, right? Uhm hmm, well you cannot have it without first giving it yourself. *(Matthew 6:14; Colossians 3:13, KJV)*

So, let's practice using those words. It will serve us well in the end because if you don't forgive others, then neither will He forgive you because, "You reap what you sow."

It's Hard

Sometimes the fleshly side of our nature does not want to forgive so readily. We may find ourselves thinking things like, "That's what they deserve!" I mean most of you have had that thought at some point or another; how could you not?

Then that voice that you do NOT want to hear speaks up and says, "Now Christian person, where is the love of the Lord in that line of thinking? Hm-m-m?" And yet an opposing voice speaks up and says, "They knew better! They need a beating! They need a good old-fashioned caning, hide tanning; they need…"

Vengeance is Mine

When that enemy that has plagued you for so long first gets hit, you are shocked. I mean, it was like they lived under some kind of shield where they could do their dirty work and never, ever get touched by anything. But then when their world starts to crumble, with first one small thing and then something greater and on and on, you feel sorry for them and pray for them with pity.

And sometimes that enemy is moved with contrition and asks you to forgive them and to pray for them, which, of course, you do. But then sometimes they never ask for forgiveness, and when a given set of trials are over, they go right back to doing the same kinds of things that they used to do to you. That is a part of life, but what that enemy does not realize is that their conscience may have been seared with a hot iron unto their own destruction. Some folk learn, and some choose not to. Some have made it such a habit of hating you and plotting your downfall that they can not break themselves of that habit. That is a horrid situation to be in, and I would not want to be them because their mistreatment of you may soon come home to roost. In other words, it may be time for their harvest of the seeds that they have sown for so long. Uh oh! Sad day.

You Pray for Them When They Get Hit

Yes, you feel sorry for them, and you pray for them. And I don't know about you, but when something like that happens to an enemy of mine, I walk gently on, a little bit in awe wondering if what your enemy is suffering has anything to do with the way they treated you. Then you think, "Nah, they were mean to so many people..." But still you wonder. And you walk on, more determined than ever to keep doing your best to live for the Lord.

Just Remember

You are never alone, even when it seems that the bottom has fallen out of your world and absolutely nothing makes any sense anymore. Yep, folks, been there, done that. But I kept going on blind faith. And I kept pushing through mistreatment with eyes glassy from recently shed tears and with fresh wounds on an already battered soul. But I knew that if I just kept my faith and just kept stepping on with one determined plant of a foot after the other, that I would reach the place that the Lord had already determined that I needed to be. And I knew that the lessons that I learned on the journey would serve me in good stead for something on down the road. Then, too, I knew that when I reached where He wanted me to be, sweet relief and rest was waiting for me.

And too, I remembered that He laughs…

Poetry Offerings for Lesson 5

Don't Make His Child Shed a Tear
Don't make His child shed a tear
When they talk to Him about you
I guarantee you won't like
What the end result will be
When He deals with you
For causing their face to be streaked
With the tears that you see.
(Psalm 72)

No Matter
No matter what my enemy wants for me
My true path lies in my destiny
Which takes me to heights heretofore unknown
To that place, God decreed to be.
Some say that what was meant to be
Has already been
But I labor under the shield of faith
That only God says when
Or if a thing is to be and so
Armed with that belief, it
Is on down the road I go.

****

I'm Sorry
Hello Bro. So-and-so or
Sis. Whatever Your Name May Be
I want to say that I am sorry for the deed done
And ask that you forgive me.

Answer to *I'm Sorry*

Okay, I forgive you for the
Wrong that you did to me
But I will never forget it, nor
Can we ever be close again
For you showed me what you were all about
When you took the trust that I placed in you
And turned that trust out!
(Is the poem above an example of genuine forgiveness?)

****

I Forgive You

Don't worry about it brother, sister, friend
I forgive you and am moving on
So, let us, both continue our trek
Toward heaven and home.

****

Wrong Done

Going around and having ill will toward someone
Is not going to accomplish anything
So why not let bygones be bygones
And maybe a soul to Christ, you will bring.

Remember, it is not about the wrong
Done to you or me
It's about a heavenly habitation…
A place to spend eternity.

****

BYDWP 2

Lift Up Your Voice

Never underestimate the power of prayer
I have seen it work on big and small
For there is not a man created that cannot fall
So, it behooves all who rise to the top
To be careful how you go and always
Carry out your duties with care
Because you don't want to be Humpty Dumpty
And topple from the wall
…and with that said, "That's all y'all!"

****

Mercy

I am glad that I have not
Been dealt with as I deserved
I am glad that justice was tendered
With mercy and that that is what I was served.

Make no mistake; it still rankles when my
Thoughts dwell on wrongs done to me
But I remember that I, too, received
A generous helping of
Mercy.

****

Harvest of Plenty

Apologizing and forgiving are key
And make a better woman of you and me
While insuring a harvest of positive plenty.
Whether you were done wrong
Or you did wrong to another, remember, fellow man
Since the beginning of time

Seeds have been sown and grown
And the reaper always collects the harvest
When He sweeps the land.

Whatever you practice day in and day out
Will be what you do and will
End up being what your life is about
For you are planting seeds on a row
So, what type of garden will you grow?

Plant plenty seeds of passing-good-deeds-forward
And plant lots of forgiveness, too
For one day the reaper will present
The crop that you have sown, to you.
****

Hard to Forgive
If you can't get over the deed
Just do what Jesus did and
See a soul in need.

You have had to be forgiven
For things you've done yourself
Then why do you feel justified
In withholding that blessing from someone else?
(Col. 3:13)
****

Discussion Questions

1. What does the scripture say about not being willing to forgive your fellowman?

_____

_____

_____

_____

2. Do all of our deeds come back to us multiplied?

_____

_____

_____

_____

3. When our enemies cause us trouble, why does God laugh?

_____

_____

_____

_____

4. According to Hebrews, what surprise might we hear at the judgment concerning our deeds?

_____

_____

_____

_____

5. Give Bible for not receiving forgiveness if you do not give it yourself.

_____

_____

_____

_____

For Further Reading
Colossians 3:13

It's Not About

It's not about the diamonds
Or about the rings
It's about the love of GOD and
The joy that HIS love brings.

It's not about houses, land
Or other acquired things
It's not about power such
As wielded by kings.

It's about living for GOD
And honoring HIS glory
It's about telling this world
The age old story
Of how Jesus died on that old tree
So that we could live with Him
Throughout all eternity.

Luke 12:15

Lesson 6:

Change in Economic Status

Scripture: Job 28:24; Job 1:10; Job 42:12

Aim: TO BE MINDFUL OF THE FACT THAT we are successful by God's grace. TO LEARN TO TRUST GOD at all times.

Song: I Will Trust in the Lord; Victory in Jesus

Living life from day to day we often work within certain parameters that may or may not be of our choosing. We learn what works for us in given situations and consequently, develop comfort zones. And we manage to do a fairly good job of living life in a modicum of comfort.

The general statement above covers several systems of constraints, be it, family, work, church, etc. Things flow smoothly in our lives as long as everything stays in its place. But sometimes things don't go smoothly, and we have to move out of our comfort zones.

You take the family budget for example. We have learned to save for several contingencies that may crop up in a family situation and usually manage to cover everything. But sometimes work may intrude in on the family budget with things like loss of overtime, etc. Then, too, your Christian duty may intrude in on the family budget. If a dire need arises in someone's life and you are the one who it is thrust upon, you may not have the necessary resources to take care of that need. But you have to, so you may end up depleting a supply source that you had managed to save even though you had been hard hit of late yourself.

What Do You Do

You find yourself in a quandary. Do you tighten your family's financial belt and step out on faith or what? I can tell you this. For the average person, no amount of preparation will make you ready for every contingency that crops up in life. Sometimes you have to bend so much that you think that you will break, but you don't. Instead, you get stronger. How does this happen? It happens by leaning on the Lord, utilizing prayer, and remembering that God always will provide.

What am I saying? I am saying that you take what little you have managed to put back and share it with someone that life has knocked down and dragged for a bit.

Dark Days

The Handlebiz's the young family that you will meet in the final

case in point for this lesson had no idea that they would lose their main bread winner, the dad, yet it happened. In the story, you see where an eight year old boy has to step up and try to help his Mom make ends meet. For our purposes today, you will meet young Pete Handlebiz and see that he has been struggling for about 8 years. He is now sixteen and manages to help his Mom eke out a living for them. Then, wham out of the blue, reduction in economic status! What do you do?

The sign above is not one that we see when our world is about to come crashing down. But remember that while nobody enjoys dark days, they are often necessary to:

- show us how good we had it in our days of light (Job 29:2-4)
- weed out false friends and show us which friends are true
- make us slow down and smell the flowers
- make us realize that we are successful in what we do by God's grace
- prepare us for blessings ahead.

Appreciate the times that your stream bubbles merrily along against the times that the current of life will flood your world with such havoc, that you don't know what to do. But remember that eventually the flood will subside, and the sun will shine again. Learn the lessons that your dark days present and be blessed.

Case in Point

When I think back to the lady who was my mother, I marvel. Listen to my story and you will see why.

My Story

She began her life in an affluent home in rural Mississippi near a place called Pace. Her daddy was well-placed in life due to the singing and sharp business acumen of his parents. I understand that they were touring musicians who saved their money until they earned enough money to buy some land. I further understand that they settled down to farm.

My mother often told me how her dad (my Grandaddy) raised hogs, vegetables, and some cows to feed the family. She told of having steaks many times during the week. She said that there were very few things that they went to town to buy. There was a peddler that used to come by selling some wares and sometimes they would be treated to some of his wares. But mostly, they ate what they raised on the farm.

She told of the idyllic days she remembered as a little girl when she and her sisters would make mud pies in the lead-crystal dishes that her mother did not care for. She often grieved over the crystal plates and bowls that her mother let them break up because she said she did not like them. We loved hearing about the days when our Momma would sit down and tell us about the way life used to be for her and her sisters. Then she would finish her reminiscing by saying that was the way it was then, but this is the way it is now. Then she would launch into her favorite tirade about falling from sugar to *!x*! The last sentence of her tirade was always, "That's why you stay in school so that you can be somebody and have something one day, so help you God."

I think she talked to me the most because I was always at home with her and because I was her only girl. At any rate, I digress. Momma's days as a carefree girl came to an end when she met and married my daddy against her Daddy's wishes. She told me that shortly after she got married, her mother fell ill from gallbladder complications and died as a result of them. My mother had only been married three months when her mother died. So, as a new bride, she had to learn to make it without advice from her mother.

Nevertheless, she carried on, doing the housewifely things that farmers wives do. She told me that it was a big day for her when her old principal drove to her house to visit her. He had come looking for her because they needed a teacher and he remembered how smart she was. After hem hawing, she told him that she would talk it over with her husband, my daddy.

She and my daddy finally came to an agreement, and she became a teacher. She taught for three years until she gave birth to my oldest brother prematurely. She said that she blamed herself for the premature birth because her sister was at her house one day and was teasing her unmercifully because she would not pick up the churn and pour my daddy some milk. She said that her sister said to her, "Child, if that was my man done come in from the field all hot and tired, I would pour him some milk." So, she did. She started hurting the minute she set the churn down and my oldest brother was born that night, a preemie.

No More Teaching

She had to give up her teaching because she did not have anyone to keep her baby.

Momma never told us how much my brother weighed at birth, but he was small enough that she worried about his even catching the sniffles. She needed someone to come to her house and take care of her baby while she taught school. She could not get anyone. Her mother was dead, and her sisters lived too far away. That's just the way it was. So, she quit her teaching job and stayed at home to provide the tender care a baby needs, especially a preemie.

She and my daddy had to move out of the new home they had just bought. They moved into a farmhouse provided for sharecroppers. This is where you work the land in return for a place to stay, a charge account for foodstuffs and other things needed on the farm, and for a small settlement at the end of the growing season. Momma had thought to go back to teaching the next school term, but a year of college was needed by then.

Again, an offer was made to her so that she could afford college, but she had no one to keep her child.

Daddy decided later to move his family to northern Mississippi, which happened not to be so close to her Daddy. Life went pretty well for them for a time, but daddy started to go to juke joints on Friday nights and to hook up with various women. Momma stayed at home with the babies, of which there were two by this time. Momma had two boys. I was still nestled in heaven getting instructions for my sojourn to earth, I suppose. Fifteen months after my brother was born, I made my entrance into the world at a little place called Collins Chapel Hospital.

****

And now, many years later, I am here telling you my story about my Momma. My Momma was a strong believer in God, and she passed that belief on to me. She taught me that things happen in life according to God's will. She taught me the value of prayer and taught me to depend on Him. She taught me that no matter what mankind says that you cannot do, it is up to the Lord. She could have let the situation with my daddy and her subsequent change in economic status sour her on life and on God, but she didn't. Instead, she elected to teach me in word and by example, to always lean on and have faith and trust in God. My Momma elected to "show and tell" about her faith in God and I, just like a sponge, soaked up whatever she taught me.

Case in Point

Here of late when I look back over my life I think, "Oo-wee, look at how far the Lord has allowed me to come!" Then I say, "Thank You, Lord. I am grateful for not only what You have done, but for Your allowing me to see your bountifulness at this moment in time."

When I was 18 years old, I was traveling on the Continental Trailways Bus. As I rode down the highway on my way back to Memphis, my hometown, I remember thinking that when I got to Memphis, I didn't have to collect but one piece of luggage, yep, one footlocker.

That was the sum of my worldly possessions. In that footlocker were my two dresses, my school shoes, and a pair of boots that I had bought with my work-study money.

I had several thoughts back during that time, but the thought that remained uppermost in my mind was the fact that the one footlocker was all I owned in the entire world.

Fast forward several years –

I'm sitting in the living room of my modest three-bedroom home pinging away on my computer as I write. As I take a glance out of the window, I can see the U.S. flag that hangs on the front porch waving in the air as the breeze causes it to rise and fall. I look at the petunias in the flower bed in the middle of my front yard and am glad that they come back every year. If I take a stroll out of my back door, I will enter the garage that houses two cars.

As far as clothes and shoes, let's just say that I have some for every season and leave it at that.

So, I have been blessed, and I know it. Have I had troubles, problems, etc.? Yes, I have, but I am focusing on being grateful for God's bounty in my life.

Affluent Home in a Nutshell

Yesteryear I had a footlocker; today I have two children, a husband, a home, and two cars. But you know what? I had God then, and I have Him now. He carries me still. And I … I'm grateful for the favor He has placed on my life. And the way that He answered my prayers (sniff).

I embraced that teaching and now move from day to day as I try to lighten folk's loads with my writing. I know that the woman, who I dub, "A Marvel of a Woman," would be proud to see what I am doing in my second career. I am living my life for Jesus and my fellowman. And I tell you this, if you have had your setbacks, and who hasn't, don't let that determine your new boundaries. You keep stepping like my Momma did and like she taught me to do, and watch the Lord make your mountains into molehills.

We, as Christians have gotten into the habit of giving our concerns to the Lord and not worrying about them anymore, right? That is true, for the most part, until we get hit with something of great magnitude, you know something that shakes our world. Circumstances that lower our economic status fall into the world-shaking category.

In that first moment that we receive news that is catastrophic to us, most of us throw caution to the winds and panic. And that is a natural enough reaction, just as long as we remember to calm down, accept the situation as it is or seems to be, and remember that we serve a God, Who can do all things. We remember that we serve a loving ***God, Who is legendary for doing the impossible through answered prayer.***

So, what do we do?

- We start praying and stop stressing as much.
- We put the situation in God's capable hands and leave Him to it, while at the same time asking for strength.
- Often during such times, we let our minds wander back through times that we felt that certain situations *(other situations in our past)* were just as impossible, and we remember with gratitude how He worked those unworkable situations out. Remembering that, makes us have renewed faith and hope for our current disastrous situation. And after praying, some more, we step on.

Just Like a Little Kid

We hand God our problems and situations and we trustingly wait for Him to fix them. We have learned to wait and have remembered not to stress.

If you have a problem that is destroying your peace of mind, take it to God. And above all, remember that He allowed the change of economic status to happen in the first place, whether a raising or lowering in placement.

Change Is Definite
(Ecclesiastes 3:1-8)

Here are two sentences that say essentially the same thing. However, one says it with a little bit of a softer touch.

Sentence 1 – Change, though sometimes jarring, is necessary.
Sentence 2 – Change, though necessary, is sometimes jarring.

So, let's look at the two sentences, but bear in mind that, as the title states, change is a natural part of life. By the mere laws of nature, we know that change is inevitable. We know this because we are born as babies, we grow up to grow old, and then we die. That is change.

- Sentence One – Change, though sometimes jarring, is necessary. This sentence could be the sterner of the two. It could be saying, "Change is a deadpan fact of life; deal with it." Or even, "So, you got rattled by the change; get a tougher skin. Get over it already. Go with the flow and live to see another day. Contrary to what you might think, life is not all about you and does not revolve around what you wish or want."

- Sentence Two – Change, though necessary, is sometimes jarring. This sentence could be saying, in a softer tone, "Yeah, I know you got jarred, but remember that all change is not jarring. It will get better."

Sentence One

Joseph, Job, and the apostle Paul all went through jarring changes that the Lord had orchestrated. Joseph had a good relationship with the Lord and maintained it.

Apostle Paul did not have a good relationship with the Lord, in fact, just the opposite. But when he was struck blind on the Damascus Road, he developed a strong, faithful relationship with the Lord.

The Apostle Paul went through a jarring change that blessed him into getting his soul saved and blessing millions of people down through the ages, to include you and me. You see, the Lord was mindful of us way back then. Paul's life change was necessary because of God's purpose.

Sometimes, as in my case, you are put through changes so that you can bless somebody else, according to God's purpose, in their time of stress (be it economic or not) by giving them hope.

I told you above that the Lord orchestrated the jarring change in Job's life. Some scholars would differ with that statement. Let's take Job's situation and break it down a little bit. When we read in Job, chapter 1, verses 8-12, we see the beginning of change being discussed for Job and the reason for it.

It seems that the Lord was proud of Job and was bragging about him to the adversary. And of course, like people so often do today, the adversary had a pat answer to try to take some of the satisfaction from the Lord because of His pride in Job. Something was said to the effect of, "Well, no wonder he is serving You so well! You have blessed all of the works of his hands…" The conversation continued, and the Lord gave the adversary leeway to touch all that Job had. The adversary, full of assurance, told God that Job would curse the Him to His face.

You should read the first chapter of the book of Job if you haven't in a while. So, even though the adversary was the one to suggest the change in Job's life, **it could NOT have happened if**

the Lord had not given permission for the change. (When you read the chapter, you will see that there were limits placed upon what could be done to Job. That is a reassuring fact for us, too.)

Sentence 2

Abraham was told by the Lord to move away from his kin. That was a big change for him, but he did it and received manifold blessings by being faithful during the move and subsequent events.

Yes, change is definite in this life, and some of it is smoothly ushered in, and some of it jars us to our very souls. What we have to remember is that "All things work together for good for those who love the Lord." (Romans 8:28, KJV)

And as you can see with Job, Joseph and Abraham and many others, staying faithful through changes will garner blessings from the Lord. Joseph was made second in command in all of Egypt; Job was blessed with twice as much as he had before, and Abraham was blessed with a child in his old age and was told that his descendants would be as innumerable as the sand on the seashore.

Even if I never understand some things that occur and have occurred in my life, I will still honor, love and trust my Maker, Who has carried me this far on my life's journey and Who is preparing a place for me so that I can be gathered back to Him.

Still Blessed and I Know It

There are some mannerisms that make us unique.

For example, I am a person who talks with her hands. I always have been. When a thing has been a part of you for so long, you do it and never even think about it. Take a look at what happened last week.

Time for a Helping Hand Testimony

We met at a friend's house to help another friend who was down on her luck and depressed to boot. And each of us was giving our little spill towards making the miserable friend feel better. When it was my turn to speak, I told her that each one of us had gone through some rough times, times when we thought that we just could not bear the problem that we were faced with any longer. The rest of the group agreed with me.

Prayer

Then I told her that through prayer and the support of loved ones and Christian friends, we made it. I told her that all of us meeting at this particular time and place meant that she was loved, too. I told her that our being there meant that we were the Lord's arms, legs, mouth, etc. Told her that because we loved Him, we had to love her.

She was feeling so lost and alone, so I went back to the fact that all of us coming together from different cities at the same time and place of our choosing for the express purpose of making her feel loved was not a coincidence. I told her that, God, in His infinite wisdom had us to come together to remind her of how much she was loved.

We managed to touch her to the extent that she was brought to grateful tears. All in all, she felt much love and felt that her situation would be resolved in due time. She resolved to begin trusting in the Lord more than ever, even when she did not understand. Of course, there were some physical needs that she had that needed to be met and we did just that.

We all came together to bless her and praise the Lord at the same time.

Mannerisms

Now back to the mannerisms that I mentioned in the first paragraph. In my zeal to make our friend feel better, I was using my hands extensively as I talked. Well, as I was talking, one of the ladies who was sitting near me, grabbed my hand and exclaimed, "Oo-wee! That is a beautiful ring!" I said, "What?" Then she said, I did not mean to cut you off, but that ring with all of that fire is gorgeous!" We all laughed a bit and then I said, "It is pretty, isn't it?" To which, they all chorused, "Yes, it is."

I never missed a beat. I said, "Uh-hmm, eleven bucks from Seattle, Washington." The one who had grabbed my hand said, "You don't mean it?" I told her that yes, I did mean it and went on to explain about the fact that it came from the Mount St. Helens eruption. One said, "Get outta here!" And another one said, well it sure is pretty, and the others are, too." I told her that people often commented on the Mount St. Helens ring because it looks just like the fieriest opal there ever was. The one who had first mentioned my ring said, "Umph, umph, umph, all that fire. You never would know it!"

God Can

Then one of the others said, "Well the red ones, they are real, aren't they?" I said, "The little one is a tiny ruby, but the larger one is just simulated. She then said, "But they are pretty, though." I said thanks and then said to our friend, "You see, if the

Lord intends for you to receive a blessing, He will orchestrate things so that you are in the right place at the right time, just like He did me with my eleven-dollar ring and you with us gathered here today expressly for your encouragement." Then I said, "You just cannot beat Him taking care of His children," to which they all agreed.

Another Point

I mentioned to my friend about all of the rings that I used to have that hard times had stripped me of and about my house fire that one of my friends mentioned during our conversation of the hour. I told her, "Yes, most people that know me know that I love rings and that I used to have some beautiful ones. But one thing about living, you never know the hardships that life will throw at you so you have to enjoy the time and things that you have while you can and continue to work for the Lord, anyhow. He is still God and I recognize Him as Such no matter how my economic status changes.

Not Things

<u>Life is not about things, but about living a life that is pleasing to God.</u> (Luke 12:15, KJV)

I told my friend that we had come to help, "You see me, don't you? The beautiful rings are gone and so is my new home, but you see me still smiling. Do you know why? I smile because I still have God's love. And if He gives me more beautiful rings, good, but if He does not, that is okay, too. He let me have them for a while, and I am thankful to have had the pleasure of wearing them for the time that He allowed me to. (Job 29:2-4, KJV) Then I smiled at her and sang a little song to plant a lasting memory in her head for those times that she might tend to become despondent again when she is alone. She started humming the song as I sang.

"Where is all of this rambling going, you might ask?" Like I told my friend, I'm still blessed, and I know it. And I can say so.

To those who are despondent, what with the cares of life and what-have-you, be encouraged and know that He cares for you and He put it on my heart today to tell you so.

To Ponder

Who would have thought that the Lord would use an eleven-dollar fiery ring from the Mt. St. Helens eruption and a mannerism such as talking with the hands to illustrate and bring home such points that He did? Only God!

Last Case in Point for Lesson 6

I needed something to cap this lesson off, so I thought that this would be a good time to give you the ending for the story that so many of you have asked me about from my prior book in the ladies inspirational series, *Chopping My Row*. If you recall, I introduced you to a young do-gooder of a hero who had taken on wearing the pants in the family upon the death of his dad some eight years prior. That meant that young Pete Handlebiz had to ride herd on his siblings, Julie and Joe, and especially his next in line brother, Bob (short for Robert).

Let's see, where were we. Oh yeah, young 16-year-old Pete had seen red when his mother came home in tears because she had been unjustly dressed down at work and fired. It probably didn't help matters that Gwendolyn Braggadocious, the daughter of Claudia Braggadocious, had been the one that ... Wait a minute, what am I doing?! It will be easier for you to follow the story if I just pick the story back up close to where we ended it in **Chopping My Row**. Okay? Good, then here we go...

Continuation of the Pete Handlebiz story from <u>Chopping My Row</u>

Pete finished scanning the local want ads. He had been hoping to find summer jobs for the boys. Pete was thankful for the three days a week delivering flowers that he had. Still, it would help if he got something that paid more money or were given more hours per week. Yet, he didn't complain. He knew that his having the delivery job was a blessing because he could drop by to check on the boys and his sister if he needed to and he saved money on lunch that way too. He sighed and was still perusing over the job situation when Julie came back in lugging her crocheting box. She had been given a kit, but Julie's work had soon needed more space and had grown to fruit box size, though Julie, bless her heart, still referred to it as her kit.

Julie placed her things just so around her and then bent to get the ripple afghan that she had just started. From upstairs, she had drug her granny square throw from her bedroom chair and her crochet on the double afghan that she had made for her bed.

"Pete," eleven-year-old Julie said.
Pete looked up and said, "What Julie?"

"I was wonderin' if I could make some throws and coverlets for some of my friends and all."

Pete had learned years before never to take anything Julie asked him for granted, so he said, "And just what does 'And all' mean?"

"Well," said Julie, sort of hem-hawing. "I wondered if I might sell some of them in the children's bazaar booth at the July 4th and Labor Day picnics?"

Pete looked at Julie, his little sis and wondered where the time had gone. He couldn't believe that she was eleven years old. It seemed like it was just yesterday that Dad had died. Pete shook himself out of his reverie and replied, "I don't know, Julie let me ask Mom about that. Okay?"

Julie said, "I hate it when you say that because you and Mom always say no to everything I want to do to help out around here. In case you both hadn't noticed, I am not a baby anymore. When Daddy died, "He didn't leave no babies!"

Pete pushed back from the table and reached Julie in one stride. He enfolded her in his arms and said, "Aw Spunkin, that's not fair."

Julie started to cry and told him about the girls in her English class talking about where they were going to go for school shopping during the summer. She told Pete that Gwendolyn Braggadocious had named all of the girls in the room that mattered. After she had done that to the whispering snickers and thumbs up from her buddies, she had proceeded to name the other girls in the room one by one. She had said that Hanna Ship was too fat to matter. The whole class had laughed at that. "But I didn't laugh because I did not think it was funny and I wondered what she was going to say when she got to me," said Julie.

Pete was wiping his sister's eyes when the boys came in from their chores, books in hand. They both stopped in the kitchen doorway and chorused, "What's wrong with Julie?"

"Nothing, a little family talk, and TLC, won't cure," Pete said gruffly.

Joe bounded into the room and grabbed a tissue out of the tissue box that was on the table and handed it to his sister, before settling himself on the sofa. Bob sat in the wing back chair that Momma always used.

"Alright guys, Mom just drove up in the driveway, so go help her bring in the food," said Pete. The boys bounced up and headed toward the glassed in area that was their front porch to stop short. Their Mom was already out of the car and she was hurriedly wiping her eyes as she turned away from the windows back toward the car. Bob, ever the sharp one said, "She looks like she's been crying."
They both turned and went back into the living room and Joe, said to Pete, "Momma's been crying, Sh-sh-sh."

When Momma came into the front room, she had four innocent looking pairs of eyes intently looking at her. She said to Julie, "Where's my hug; can't a momma get a hug around here today?" To which all of her children responded, and she ended up in a big bear of a group hug.

Julie's voice was heard from within the group hug, "Momma, why were you crying?"

The boys yelled, "Julie."

Momma shushed each one of them and told them all to sit down. Then she said, I have some bad news, children.

Bob piped up, "I hope it don't mean that I don't get my x-box for my birthday."

Pete cleared his throat and grunted under his breath and said, "What is it Momma that has made you cry?"

"It's nothing that a little extra effort from all of us won't remedy. It's just that Claudia Braggadocious used my computer after hours yesterday and sent out some unflattering emails about the boss' wife. The boss' wife came to the office today, and we all could hear her crying from his office. When she left, she gave me a red-eyed, malevolent stare and hissed as she passed me that she had been nothing but good to me. Then her husband called me into his office and fired me after yelling at me. He was so mad when he called me in, that he slammed his office door so hard that it bounced back open, and all of the office got to hear him dress me down. I was so humiliated that I could not hold my head up as I packed my things."

Momma sat down on the arm of the couch and finished drying her tears and said, "But that is that. What we have to do is figure out how to make ends meet until I can get another job. Pete, I didn't stop by the store on my way home. Do you kids think that you can eat the remainder of yesterday's spaghetti for dinner?"

"Sure we can; can't we troop," said Joe.

When Momma headed to the bathroom to freshen up, Pete who had not said a word, looked at Bob and said, "You are in charge until I get back. Make sure everybody gets the same amount of spaghetti. Me? Don't worry about me. I ate on the truck today." Pete went upstairs and came back down with his steel baseball bat and banged out of the door. He was muttering under his breath about seeing a liar about a lie and a bonehead about a bone.

Momma came out of the bathroom to see him tearing down the road in her car. All she could do was wring her hands because she had never learned to drive that old stick of Pete's that had belonged to her husband. Momma got on the phone and called her brother, Justin, in Toledo, who lived 200 miles away.

Now ladies, I bet somebody is sitting there thinking, "Oh Boy! What is he going to do? Lawd have mercy; I hope he doesn't let them get him into trouble!"

Have you ever known someone to be in the grips of justifiable anger like Pete is in? I'm pretty sure that you have. My question to you is, " What's he going to do with that bat?!" Oh my, this youngster has his whole life ahead of him. Oh dear! Oh dear! Tee hee Gotcha going don't I? Well, keep reading and let's see what happens...

Pete was so angry that he could see red. He was angry with his dad for dying; he was angry with Claudia Braggadocious and her snooty daughter; he was angry at life for making a sixteen-year-old do a man's job; but most of all, he was angry with Benny Grabrun for firing his mother without checking the facts.

Pete thought about the last time that he had seen red. That had been years ago, about a week after his dad's funeral. His brother, Bob had sassed his mother something awful because she had told him for the fifteenth time to turn his television off and go to sleep. When he had refused, his mom had marched into the boys' room and had yanked the TV cord out from the wall so hard that it had bent the prong on the plug.

That was when Bob, probably because he was grieving, had said that he hated her. His mom had replied, "Join the club; life hates me too." Pete would always remember the way his mom had run past his room sobbing. Pete remembered that he had said out loud, "Daddy, why did you go and leave us like this?" He had lain in his bed listening to his mom sobbing. When things had gotten quiet in her room, Pete had made a pretend trip to the bathroom. When he tiptoed past his mom's room, he could hear the quiet even sound of her breathing. Every now and then she would hiccup in her sleep.

Pete had been on his way back to his room when he saw light coming from under his brothers' door. Pete had opened the door and had seen Bob watching TV. Pete had said to Bob, "You turn that TV off right now and if you ever make my mom cry again, I will beat you up within an inch of your life." Bob had said, "You ain't my dad." Pete saw red! Before he realized what he was doing, he had hit his brother with a round off kick and knocked him down, and had his knee pressing against Bob's windpipe. That had been when Joe, who had been quietly watching the whole thing, had jumped up and said, "Top it Pete, Top! You gonna git 'em dead!"

Pete had let Bob up. Then he had said to Bob, "The TV stays off for a week. You got me? And if you ever make my Momma cry again, I'll beat you Bob and you know I can!" Joe scurried to turn the TV off! Bob, who had been gasping for breath, said, "She my momma, too." To that Pete snarled, "Then act like it."

Pete had vowed then, that he would never lose his temper like that again and he never had. He had never seen red again until today. While clenching the metal bat, he gunned the car through the traffic light that had just turned red...

You know that we left off with Pete gunning his mother's car through a red light on his way to the newspaper office that his mother had just gotten fired from. You do remember that he was livid? Yes, I know you remembered that he brought a steel bat with him.

(Here we come upon the scene with Pete, driving his mother's car. Hold on everybody, we got a curve coming up. I tell you what, if young Pete doesn't slow down, he won't need a steel bat nor anything else. Y'all all in? Good now buckle up those seat belts! The ride might get a tad bumpy.)

Pete squealed into the parking lot and jumped out of the car with his steel bat in his hand. He took the stairs leading to the press office two steps at a time. When he got to the top of the stairs, he met the lady that he had privately dubbed, "The stink stirrer of the newspaper (gossip columnist)" coming out of the press office.

Pete gestured with the bat and motioned with his other hand for her to do an about face. When he got her back inside the office, he heard someone say, "Oh, shoosh!"

Pete gestured for the gossip columnist to sit down at her desk and said, "Take note; you might get something juicy for your column."

The gossip columnist sat down at her desk with her eyed bucked and mumbled to herself, "This is gonna be good."

(Meanwhile, back at home...)

Momma got her brother's voicemail and left an urgent message asking him to call her back and send up an urgent prayer for Pete, who had taken a steel baseball bat into her former office to, as he put it, "See a liar about a lie and a bonehead about a bone."

Bob, who had been telling his mom to hang up all while she was dialing her brother, said, "Mom!"

"What are you yelling about, Robert? And there is no need to yell. I'm right here."

Bob said, "Mom, you don't understand! Pete will kill somebody. He gets crazy when somebody makes you cry."

Mom said, "I don't believe you and don't you ever speak about your brother like that again; you hear me?!"

Joe said, "Mom, Robert is right. Pete will kill somebody for making you cry. We can talk about it in the car. Right now, we have to save Pete."

Mom wailed, "I can't drive Pete's car!"

Bob said, "I can; I've seen Pete do it many times."

Bob had trouble getting the engine to start, it kept going dead. Julie started crying. Joe was praying aloud.

Mom yelled at Bob, "Robert Handlebiz, you get this mangy contraption started and you get it started right now! I don't intend for some mangy liar to cost me my oldest son!"

Bob yelled at the old car, "Listen, you lily-livered son of a flea-bitten gumshoe! You start and you start right now, or I'll go under your hood and yank some parts and you will be an automatic and run like a top. Do you understand me?! One of the troops own is in trouble!"

The car started like a well-run engine and sputtered a couple of times on the way, but that was it.

On the way over to the newspaper, Joe told the story of how Pete had kicked Bob and had put his knee on his throat and told him that if he ever made you cry again, he would beat him within an inch of his life. He meant it, too, Mom. I had to pull him and his legs trying to get him off Bob."

Mom said, "Hurry Bob! Can't you go any faster?! Stop crying, Julie and start praying; Joe, go back to praying! Everybody, pray!"

The Handlebiz's were a praying troop that day. When they got to the newspaper office, Mom's car was parked taking up two lanes. The driver's door was open, and the engine was still running. Bob let Joe, Julie, and Mom off beside Mom's car and parked Pete's truck downslope against the guard rail on the other end of the parking lot. He switched the key off and the truck quit after a little rattle. He took off at a run and caught up with his mom and the rest of the troop.

(Meanwhile, inside the office…)

Pete said, "Okay, everybody since I have your attention, I have an announcement to make."

Nobody moved a muscle. He said, while looking at the lady who had backed into the office with him, "Now your job is gossip columnist, is that right?" She nodded her head, "Yes."

"Did you know that Claudia Braggadocious and her daughter spend every summer living with poor relatives on the east coast so that they can go to all of the ritzy yard sales and estate sales for clothes and what-have-you? Did you know that they sell what clothes that they cannot pass off as new and also shop regularly at newly new shops so that her prating-long-necked fake daughter can come back home here and try to high and mighty it over the women and girls of this town? Did you get that GC?"

"I got every last word of it."

A lady in the back stood up and said, "I don't think that is any of my business, so please excuse me," and started to walk toward the back room.

She had taken two steps when Pete brought the steel bat down on top of the conference table with a wham and roared, "Sit down, all of you!"

The lady scrambled back to her seat and stayed there. Somebody said from the back, "I ain't taking this for the likes of Claudia Braggadocious. Yeah, she typed on your mother's computer because I came back in the office for something I had forgotten, and I saw her typing there. The light was on in your Mom's cubicle and I was going to turn it off but I saw Claudia typing there and eased on back out. I did wonder what all the hullabaloo was about. I just got back to the office thirty minutes ago and have spent that time typing what I saw in an email to Mr. Bonegrab. He's out of the office right now, so he may not have had time to read it."

Somebody piped up and said, "He is back in his office from lunch now because I heard his personal door chime."

Just then, Mr. Bonegrab's inner office opened, and he stepped through demanding, "What in thunderation is going on?"

At the same time, the outer office door opened and the rest of the Handlebiz's poured into the office. Bob said, "Pete, are you alright?"

Mom said, "Son, let me handle it. You are only a sixteen-year-old."

Pete responded to his mom, "Mom, you don't know how I wish that were true."

The boss said, "For the love of Pete, will somebody tell me what in blue blazes is going on and why she (gesturing at Pete's Mom) is here."

Claudia stood up and said, "I didn't mean no harm, I was only funning a bit. I never meant to send it and I did not put your mother's name on it. It was all in fun."

The same reporter from the back said, "Another lie. You know good and well that when an email is typed on any computer in this office, it attaches the name of the person whose workstation that is. Please "Princess" Claudia, don't insult us."

The lady who wanted to leave earlier yelled out, "You need to check your email from the last thirty minutes, Mr. 'B.'"

Mr. Bonegrab said to Pete, "It seems that I made a hasty judgment without looking into all of the facts. Please let's go into my office and discuss this in private. There has been enough damage done today. Pete, I owe your mother and the rest of your family an apology and I would like to make it up to you. If you would be man enough to take your family into my office, I will be there shortly. There is some trash here that I have to dispose of."

Well, readers, young Pete was saved from ruining his life and all seems to be well. Whew, I am, glad that he did not ruin his life. And that lady, all in fun, yeah, right!

Well, when situations like this crop up in life, we all will just have to try to handle it in a modest way as a Christian ought and not allow our light to go dim, even when our finances are made slim because of another's whim.

With the help of Mr. Bonegrab and his wife, Pete's Mom went on to become a partner in the newspaper, Julie to marry and open her own Knitting,Crochet/Fabric Shop, Bob to own a chain of automobile parts stores, Joe to become a vet and Pete to become a city councilman, mayor and governor of the state.

Poetry Offering for Lesson 6

Well, Well, Well

There are times that bring life changing catastrophic news
That seem to stroll with leisure through your life
Often taking up residence, it seems
Then there are happy times that are so fleeting
That you wonder if and when there'll be another meeting.

But what can always be counted on is
The fact that nothing lasts forever whether good or bad
And you have to learn to make the most of the good times
And ride out the ones that make you sad.

So, savor the good times and make sweet memories
That will help you through when you have those times that
Make you shake your head and say
"Well, well, well," or "Umph, Umph, Umph."
— Always remember that these, too, shall pass away.

Ecclesiastes 3:1-8

****

Sometimes You Get Tired

Sometimes you get tired
Sometimes you get worn
Sometimes you feel like you're walking
On your journey all forlorn.

Then faith takes a stand and reminds you

Of the road you've traveled so far
How you felt just as bereft back then
And yet, HE brought you through.

So fellowman, pass that microphone
To faith a little more often
Then that bitter shell of disillusionment and weariness
Through faith's coaching, will begin to soften.

Matthew 11:27-29

Get Back Up

Have you ever felt that
You got hit the hardest
Whenever your life was going well
You had all your angles figured out
And you were making all kinds of strides
Then trouble reared its ugly head
And from the top of the ladder you fell?

Well, you'll just have to pick
Yourself up and dust yourself off
And start your climb again with
Your feet shod with the preparation
Of the gospel of peace and your
Head covered with the helmet of salvation.

In short, you need to equip yourself
With the whole armor of GOD
(Christian battle gear)
Which you can read about in

Lift Up Your Voice

Ephesians chapter 6, verses 13-18
Then you can deal with whatever
The adversary puts on you
Without resorting to hating
And without giving in to fear.

Eph. 6:13-18

****

*I know that He will continue to take care of me, regardless of
the ebb and flow of the changes in life and I always remember
that This too, just like time, shall pass away...*

Discussion Questions

1. What scripture implies that change in our economic status cannot happen without God's permission?

_____

_____

_____

_____

2. What does Luke 12:15 say about material abundance?

_____

_____

_____

_____

3. What scripture says that nothing lasts forever, whether good or bad?

_____

_____

_____

_____

4. What does Ephesians 6:13-18 admonish to do?

_____

_____

_____

_____

5. ___God, is legendary for doing the impossible through answered prayer.___ What should this bold printed phrase mean in the life of a Christian?

_____

_____

_____

For Further Reading
Psalm 102:26; Philippians 4:6-7; 2 Corinthians 4:16-18; Job 31:4

When We No Longer Walk
When we no longer walk this earthbound plane
The legacy we build will still remain.

Lesson 7:

This Thing That You Do

Scripture: Matthew 5:14-16; 2 Timothy 3:12-17; 1 Peter 5:7; Proverbs 3:5; Philippians 2:15

Aim: TO LEARN TO APPRECIATE THE LOVE OF GOD and be joyful for it. TO BE MINDFUL OF THE FACT that we are in the spotlight at all times and may have it fully trained upon us at any given moment, so it is important what we do. TO BE MINDFUL OF THE FACT that though we suffer the fiery trial of persecution and storms, to remember that, at all times, we are in God's hands.

Song: A Beautiful Life

In a Positive Way

A long time ago, I decided that if I could write something to help someone in a positive way, either by giving them escape through the book page, blog or through a touching verse, then that was what I would do. I had a teaching colleague to tell me several years ago, that my work would linger on long after I was gone. She said that it was of the caliber to stand the test of time. Those sincere words of hers made my day and, from time to time, inspire me as I work to serve out my life mission of praising my God and encouraging and inspiring my fellowman.

Somebody Because of Whose Representative You Are

What comes to your mind when you hear the word, ambassador? An official representative of a country or cause is what comes to my mind. However, I looked the term up on Wikipedia and here is what it said:

An ambassador is an official envoy, especially a high-ranking diplomat who represents a state and is usually accredited to another sovereign state or to an international organization as the resident representative of their own government or sovereign or appointed for a special and often temporary diplomatic assignment. (https://en.wikipedia.org/wiki/Ambassador)

I like the portion of the definition where it says, *"resident representative of their own government… appointed for a special and often temporary diplomatic assignment."* Do you know what that means to us if we are children of God? It means that we are **somebody** special, that we are resident representatives of Heaven's government, that we have been given a temporary assignment to carry out, and that we have the backing of the Government of Heaven!

Did you know that you **are somebody because you walk and talk for God?** Can you even conceive of the idea?! Wow! I, for one, never thought about my Christian walk in that manner. I just thought of it as a work that I am committed to because of my love for the Lord.

I now realize that because He deemed me worthy to die for, I really am somebody, no matter what any man or woman thinks about me. I have been given a job of the utmost importance, that of saving men's souls. Umph, me with the job of saving souls, souls, mind you, the most precious commodity in this world!

Since I realize what a precious commodity I have been entrusted with, I wonder if I am up to the task. That is a big job for a big **somebody**. Hey, wait a minute, that **somebody** given the job is me!

When You See Me Coming

What is love? Is it a warm feeling of well-being, a heart throbbing pulsation at the approach of a certain one, etc.? It can carry different connotations depending on the way it is used. For our purposes today, love is being used to mean an expression of brotherly concern for others.

Wouldn't it be wonderful if when people saw you coming, they said or thought, "Here he/she comes,"? We know what is on their mind, Jesus."

Why Jesus, because Jesus is love and love is what it took to get us back into the correct relationship with GOD.

When you see me coming, I will have, "Being about God's business on my mind." That is a powerful statement to make, but it is an even more powerful one to live.

When You See Me Coming

That statement means maintaining love for
Mankind whether folks love me back or not
It means loving folks when they smile or when they frown
It means loving folk when they let it be
Known that they don't want me around.

When you see me coming just know that I see
Another one of God's creations, an earthen vessel just like me
To be greeted with a smile and a cheery, "How are you?"
Being mindful of the fact that though on different levels
Of our journey, we both are trying to make it through.

Living My Life

"I like living this kind of life; it is the blessed (best) life." This
sentence is the first line of a song sang by the Clark Sisters and,
you know, the words ring true for me. What life am I referring to,
why the life of living for the Lord, of course. I like living for Him
because He allowed His Son to die for me. I like living for Him
because He claims me in front of all creation. He allowed His
Son to die for me so that I could be sanctified and brought back
to the safety of the fold. And this God, the Creator of the world,
has allowed me to serve Him in His majesty. He has placed His
Spirit within me so that His glory can shine through me daily, as I
live for Him. Ah, this is the life.

I get joy out of serving Him as I look forward to the hope of
glory. I get excited when I get to brag on Him to others because I
know that I am carrying on with the mission that He had in mind
before the world began. I get excited to think that I am being
allowed to play a part in His great plan. That is an awesome
thought, folks. The Creator of this world has and is allowing me
to help carry out some of His plans, and I like it! He does not

need me to do this because He has countless others that will and are doing the job. But because He loves me, and cares about my contentment, He allows me to help, too.

I like the various jobs that He finds for me to do. If you have small children or have had small children, then you know what I am talking about. You know when you have a toddler who wants to help trim the Christmas tree, but is in the way more than he is helping, but to keep him contented and occupied, and feeling good about himself, you allow that little one to help? That is the part that I feel that I play in my work for my Father. I tell you, Folks, I am proud to serve Him.

I like:
- Speaking a kind word to someone in His name
- Giving someone a smile, in His name
- Feeling His love in the warmth of the sunshine on a crisp autumn day
- Trying to give back for His great expression of love for me
- Reveling in the knowledge of His love.

In short, I love Him and all that He stands for and am proud to tell anybody who will listen about the majestic Worker of Wonders I serve. I know that I cannot tell it all, but I do so love trying!

Many of you feel the same way I do, so we can say in unison:

"We like a Christian life
And being claimed as His own
We like serving Him and we try
To make the fact that we do, known!"

Happy Birthday

Happy birthday, if today is your birthday, that is. You will probably spend a portion of the day doing what folk usually do on their birthdays. But for our purposes here today, I want to look upon each dawn that we awaken as a birthday. Each day that we awaken, we have the privilege of seeing time give birth to a new day, in that our lives have been spared for a while longer.

Now

On this new day that we have been allowed to see, what good thing can we do? It may be something that we have done before, or it may be an extension of the work that we have already begun. It could be that we:

- put stars back in an old woman's eyes
- gladden someone's dreary existence
- provide a coat for a child's chilled back
- buy a pair of shoes to get someone's feet off of the ground
- donate a package of socks to a homeless shelter
- or any number of other things.

Remembering that our journey is not complete, we realize that there is so much more that we can do, need to do, and must do. This means that we must work on our habits by accentuating and escalating the positive ones and eradicating and diminishing the negative ones. *(Philippians 2:15, KJV)* Yes, we must remember that our deeds are recorded in the book of life and in the lives or our fellowmen through their watching us. It is so important what we do! And as always, let's remember to BYDWP because prayer sets the tone for how you handle your day because you ask

the Lord to be with you in all that your day brings.
Here is a poem that fits in with the train of thought of this piece.

A New Day
Another day closer
To my journey's end
Yet, even then I know
That I finish to begin.

This Thing that You Do

And just understand and know that if we are on a mission for the
Lord, we are going to have trouble. It goes with the job
assignment. Why are we going to have trouble? Easy, Jesus had
trouble, didn't He, and we strive to be Christlike. Besides the
Bible tells us, "All who live godly shall suffer persecution." (2
Timothy 3:12-17)

In Lesson 3, we said that it matters how you handle your adverse
times in life. We will discuss why now.

We all know that as surely as we were born, we are going to die.
(Genesis 3:19, KJV) So let us do all we can to help our
fellowman while we can. It is better to do that than to be like the

rich man in Luke 16:28, KJV, who wanted someone to tell his brothers not to come to the place where he was.

Why?

Apparently, knowing that they lived the same type of life that he did when he was on earth, he wanted them to be warned to change their ways so that they did not have to come to his place of torment.

If we live our lives as best we can as an example of a caring Christian soldier who steadily marches on, we can rest assured that our lives will have an impact on many who pass our way, including our loved ones. Now you know why I tirelessly write books and a blog everyday…somebody is blessed by what I have been given to say. In short, I care. Start your more positive legacy today.

Now we talked about how to handle ourselves when we are in trouble; let's talk about some reasons for trouble in the first place. Why do we have to have rainy days, storms, and fiery trials. (You might be wondering why I did not put this section on trouble in with the lesson that deals with storms and rainy cycles in our lives.) I did not put this treatise in the lesson that deals with storms because I wanted to bring it home to you in this Lesson entitled "**This Thing that You Do**," that it _really does matter about this thing that you_ do because no matter what action that you decide to take, somebody somewhere is watching you and thinking about emulating you. *(Matthew 5:16, KJV)*

We mentioned earlier that we have been taught all of our lives about the lovingkindness of God and how He knows all about us and any situations that occur in our lives, about how He steps in to save us when we are in trouble and provides for our needs.

We heard all of that from various older folk that we happened to be around, family, church members, etc. **But!** When that storm or rainy season hits our lives and stays around long enough that we despair of ever seeing the sun again, stays around long enough that we call, and I mean *sho' nuf* call on God, then, we begin to know the Lord's lovingkindness and saving power for ourselves after He brings us out.

It is then that we take the next step in our rainy day cycle in that we thank Him and start to talk about the greatness of the God that we serve and His lovingkindness. And we start to tell about how He, in His infinite wisdom, provides!

Say What?

Yep, just look at that! That rainy season has drawn us closer to God and created a file in our memory banks labeled, I Learned From My Storm:

- God – Unconditional love, care, and provision.

Under that, there might be a tag that says,
- *Has my back to a degree that nothing and no one else can!*

Another tag might say,
- *Greatest thing in my life, this lovingkindness.*

Still, another might say,
- *"Must tell my children and other family about Him."*

This relationship is one that we cherish and never want to be without again, a keeper. So our rainy seasons make us know, remember, and tell about the Lord. Remember verse 2 in Psalm 107 says, "Let the redeemed of the Lord say so." And remembering the grip that the storm had on us and how it felt to be delivered has us telling our story of deliverance to God's glory. Hallelujah, **what a blessing there was in that storm!** And you wondered what was the purpose of all of the pain that you went through. Now you know**...you have a story to tell.**

Yes, we all have stories of storms in our lives that we can tell to the glory of God. So, I wrote mine down to share with others about how the Lord will provide for you and bring you through. What have or are you doing with yours? Hmm-m?

Not Yet

Those of you, who have not experienced a rainy season yet, just keep living, you will. But when you do, remember the last verse of Chapter 107 of the book of Psalms which says:

> *43 Who is wise? Let him give heed to these things,*
> *And consider the lovingkindnesses of the Lord.*

That verse encourages you to know that you have an advocate with the Lord and that God will take care of you if you give your heart and soul into His keeping. He is saying to you, "You may not know me yet, but think on the fact that I have a record of being faithful and of taking care of my children. I am here for you just waiting for you to come to me in humbleness and prayer. I am the God of your mother, daddy, sister, in fact, the God of all of those that you have heard bragging on me. And yes, I am Alma's God."

Who Did That

And the last thing that I will mention today is the fact that not all storms are sent by the Lord, but all are allowed. I know, you are thinking, "Say that again. I don't quite understand what you are saying." Alright, I will. I am saying that some storms are sent to you because you have gotten the attention of the adversary. He sees your dedication to God, and He wants to try to make you turn your back on the Lord.

You don't believe me? Well, remember Job. In that book of the Bible, God was talking to the adversary about Job and was bragging on how steadfast Job was. The adversary did not like the fact and told the Lord that Job was only faithful because of all the blessings that the Lord had given him. You can read the story for yourself, but I will call your attention to the Bible in Job Chapter 1, verse 19, where a storm was sent and destroyed the house where all of Job's children were. Only a servant escaped to go back and tell Job. "What a horrible, horrible storm," you might say. Bless his heart, Job suffered from the occurrence of a literal and a spiritual storm, but he had given his soul into the care of the Lord.

And I agree, yes it was a horrible storm. But I want you to look at verse 2 of Chapter 4 of the book of Job, which says,

> ***So the Lord said to Satan "Behold, he is in your power, only spare his life."***

In a Storm But in His Hands

Those are some powerful words and bear storing in your memory. In other words, God said, "You can touch him, but don't you kill him! You will see that he is not serving me for what I can do for him, but because he is faithful to Me." What a powerful testimony to have in your favor, for God Himself to brag on you! That, my friend, is something else that may come as a result of rainy seasons and storm seasons in our lives. As I have been saying throughout this series of lessons,

From your storm learn
And your blessings earn.

And remember that God is looking, baby
And He has been looking all along
So, He's gonna keep you strong.

****

Rough Side of the Mountain

Revelation 7:9 says, "There will be a great multitude which no man can number made up of all nations… standing before the throne clothed in white robes." And Revelation 7:14 says that "It will be a number that no man can number and the people will have come through great tribulation." That's what I think about when my struggles get to be too much, so much so that I sing one of my favorite songs, "Rough Side of the Mountain," by Reverend F.C. Barnes. (You can listen to many versions of this powerful spiritual on YouTube.) And I keep stepping on doing the best I can determined to be one of that number that makes it in.

As I come to grips with being the last of my Momma's children left, I realize that I am in a position that I have never been in before, no siblings. But I am not downhearted because the myriad of first cousins that I have, reach out to me like never before. I receive texts, phone messages, and calls daily. For that, I thank them, and, too, my church family.

And though sometimes the terrain that we must travel over in our lives gets difficult, like the mountain that I am now climbing, the

Lord has let us know that we are never alone. (1 Peter 5:7) When I awake in the mornings now, I am more determined than ever to make a difference in the lives of my fellowman.

Since my writing began, I have written under the mantra of, "Doing What I Can, While I Can." And I am ready to go further and do more. Having said that, I am stepping up the writing of my next books.

Never Alone

Any decision we make in life can affect someone else. I cannot say it enough. People make judgments and form opinions about what they see you do or not do. That means that you may influence someone and not even realize it. For instance, if your mail carrier is used to seeing you day after day, picking up your mail each morning, and for several mornings you do not, that will create enough concern in him for him to mention it to someone. He may mention it to the newspaper boy, the old retired gentleman down the street or your neighbor and slight acquaintance from the house next door.

Now the reason for your not getting the mail might be something as benign as having gone on vacation or something as serious as your having fallen in the home.

The point that I am trying to make is that we must never think that what we do is our business and our business alone. Whether you have family or not, there is somebody that watches you daily and admires you. It could be the paperboy, the pizza delivery person, some neighborhood child or some child at your church, etc.

Whatever your leadership lot is in life, be it great or small, always remember to lead in a positive manner and a positive direction because somebody follows you and holds you in high regard. Here is a poem I wrote with this thought in mind.

Torchbearer
You bear not the torch for naught
You bear it for saints long gone
Who for the Savior's cause fought
In hopes of spreading the glow of His love
To encompass all mankind, yes
You bear not the torch for yourself alone
But for the glory of God
Who hails from Heaven above..

****

Case in Point - At This Time

I had just finished giving a speech to a group of young people at a Black history program. I remember that I used several examples from my life to bring my message home to them that with the Lord as the Head of their lives, nothing was impossible for them. Often, when you speak for a group, you wonder how well you did and that was the case with this engagement, too. Apparently, I need not have worried about how I did because the following paragraph is what I was told as a result of the speech.

A woman told me that day that she was proud to know me. I looked at her in such a puzzled manner that she explained what she meant. She said, "I can see that I surprised you by what I said, nevertheless, it is true. It is an honor to know you. You have so much to give to others and you don't hold back. In any situation that you are a part of; you give your all. It is a blessing and an honor to know you!" I mildly told her, "Thank you, but the glory belongs to God," and tried to sidle away without toppling off of the pedestal that she had just placed me upon. She stopped me from sidling away and said, "See, that is something else about you; you give all you have and remain so humble in doing it." I again gave her my thanks and scooted. I needed to get someplace and just breathe and think.

Only Me
I mean, it was only me,
Not some big celebrity!
She told me that people got paid thousands of dollars for
What I had just given those children for free!
I told her that it was just the glory of
God shining through me.

My Point Is

As we go about our business and do what we do, let's make the places and times in our lives count because we never know when we are setting someone on their future course or when we are molding someone for greatness. Then too, we may be spurring someone on to finish a project that they have grown weary with and feel too drained to complete. We just never know, do we?

You take what happened to me the other day, I cried! I had just finished the manuscript that I had been putting finishing touches on for several few weeks, yea! But that is not why I cried. I cried because at that moment I received a shoutout from a former student who received his Dr. of Physical Therapy Degree. Though the gesture got me teary-eyed, it brought back to the front on my mind that **the things that we do matter very much.**

Just Something to Ponder –
Words are powerful; handle with care

Because you are going to give an account for
Every word that we uttered when we get over there.

Never Forget

Never forget that He is in control. Sometimes we tend to forget
that we are not in control of our own lives. We have to be
reminded that we live, we move, and we have our being, by the
grace of God. *(Acts 17:28, KJV)* You know, there are some
people that we meet who are destined to do great things for the
Lord. Sometimes, these people who are destined to do great
things for the Lord do not even know it themselves. Think about
all of the great inventors, and statesmen in history; think about
Moses, Joseph, David, Abraham, Noah, etc. in Biblical history.

I wonder if they felt different from other children when they were
young. And I wonder if they were often ostracized because of
being different. We know that Joseph was.

You might be thinking, "What is your point?" My point is that
when you see someone who is different, be careful how you deal
with them. They may have been hand-picked for whatever by the
Lord.

On the Other Hand, If You
If you are one of those people who does things a bit differently
from others, don't sweat it. Don't put yourself down or hold
yourself back for others to like you. If you have been picked to
do a job, then go about doing it gladly. Others will come around
or they won't, but you, my friend, will know that you have
fulfilled the dream that was driving you – that dream that just
would not go away no matter how hard you tried to ignore it.

There is a reason for the persistence of your dream. Think about it!

Banging the Pots and Pans

Never forget nor take for granted the influence of a godly mother. The banging of pots and pans is a sound that brings good thoughts and feelings to mind. I remember being under my Momma's feet in her kitchen until she gave me a spoon and a pot to play with while she fixed dinner. I can still call up the loving looks and words that she used as she did her work. Ah, the sweet memory of a true mother's love…

Today I am a woman grown who is a grandmother myself with my Momma having been gone these several years. Yes, she is gone but the love she had for me will carry me until we meet again.

When I think about the love that she had for me, I think about all of the things that she did for me to make sure that I had a proper foundation rooted and grounded in love. As I am the only girl, you know that we were extraordinarily close, and for that I am thankful. My Momma used to tell me that I was *"petted to death."* I was not spoiled because that would mean an overabundance of material things. That was not the case in my childhood home.

However, I was the type of child who cried easily and expected things to be put *aright* when I did. And they usually were. So, you can imagine my joy when told about an invisible Friend, Who unlike Santa Claus, was real! That was the way I thought about Jesus then and still do now. Of course, time and circumstance have dictated that I learn that tears do not solve everything and that sometimes the way things are meant to be is not necessarily the way I would like for them to be.

When life grabs my world and gives it a resounding shake, I take refuge under the *pots and pan care* that Momma instilled in me years ago. Here is what I mean. She had me in the kitchen with her so that she could keep an eye on her baby as she prepared her dinner for the family. That way she could get her dinner done and watch the baby, too. Yes, I basked in the benevolent love that she showered me with as she worked.

Stick a pin in this one, Y'all! *(Remember)* <u>As Christians who have chosen to give our lives to the Lord and actively work in His vineyard, we can be likened to the baby that I was so many years ago!</u> Here's how. God has this whole world to watch over and keep going, etc. He does not necessarily need us to do His work for Him because He can always find someone else, even if He has to turn rocks into men. But because He cares for us and sees that we earnestly want to work for Him, He gives us some pots and pans to beat on while He continues with running this world. That is the way that I look at it, anyway. He lets me get in the fray and do the best that I can while keeping a benevolent eye on me. I am under the watchful eye of my Father, just like I was under the watchful eye of my Momma.

Making It Clear

Don't you see? I can bang the pots and pans with my spoon as much as I want to because the God that my Momma taught me about is looking at me with lovingkindness. I can make my noise for Him and He delights in my doing so. (Jeremiah 9:24) I think that He likes the fact that I want to do something for Him. That is my take on our relationship to God. What about you? Don't you just love knowing that the most powerful Force in this world is keeping watchful and protective eyes on you? I do.

For those of you who didn't get my analogy, look at it like this; It is like a little cub being protected by the Momma bear. Yep, you got that one didn't you?! Much love to you all as we continue our march toward eternity.

Learning to Lean

"Trust in the Lord with all your heart and lean not on your own understanding. "(Proverbs 3:5, KJV)

That verse says that it is a natural thing to lean on what you know. It says that though you think you know all about what is good for you and about how to handle things, there will be times when that just will not be so. There will come a time, when the Lord deems it so, that you will learn to lean on Him because your self-leaning post will be broken.

When that time comes, you will have to, against your natural self-sufficiency, realize that you need something that you cannot supply. When the "rubber meets the road" in your life, you will learn how to depend on the Lord. You will learn to be still and you will learn to know. (Psalms 46:10)

Here is the beautiful thing about learning to lean on Him. While you are leaning you are resting, gaining strength and being prepared for a victory that you may not realize is coming. But God does.

Everybody likes winning and when you stop trying to do it all yourself and ever making a bigger mess, you will learn to see how the Lord God brings victory. *(Lesson 2 revisited again)* How sweet it is, oh, how sweet 'twill be!

Joy is something that is hard to hide. If there is joy in a person's heart, you will be able to tell it. It might show in the twinkle in an eye, an ever-ready smile, the patting of a foot, the humming of a tune, the wearing of a huge grin, a bouncy walk, skipping, a jovial greeting, etc. But that is something that is hard to have when life has a go at you, isn't it? Yes, it is, but the good thing about joy is that it is contagious!

One of the things that I have decided to try to do more of this year is to look for joy and happiness in the smallest things because the big things will take care of themselves. Here's is how I propose to go about this:

- Start by being thankful. *(Being thankful helps you to see just how blessed you are.)*
- When I tend to want to whine, I am going to remember to just take a good look down the road.
- Sing a song to myself. *(It has been proven that singing naturally elevates your mood by producing positive hormones.)*
- Get a new potted plant.
- Go for a good nature walk and *take time to smell the flowers, literally and figuratively.*
- Look for *"the positive"* in situations that are not so positive.

- Choose joyful people to align myself with.
- Look for joy in all things, then that joy will help others. (Folk will look to you, just so they can hear a kind word, see a smile, etc.)

By being joyful, I can make my environment a *"feel-good place"* for all to be in. It is hard to stay moody and mean around a cheerful and joyful person. As we continue to move through this life, let us spread the love by showing joy. Afterall, every little bit helps.

All Your Might

1. The whims and desires of those destined to be great pale when compared to the needs of the world – the people they were created to serve.

OR

2. Those destined to be great often forgo their whims and desires in deference to the needs of the world – the people they were created to serve.

The two statements above convey the same meaning though they are expressed from slightly different perspectives. Statement number one suggests that because a person was born with a special gift or talent to an extraordinary degree, the talent belongs to the world; after all for the good of the world is why they possess said talent in the first place. This statement might be said by a pragmatist or by a person that could very easily become a hater.

Statement number 2 above could be uttered by a person who possesses such a talent or by a family member or close associate of one who possesses such a talent.

While both statements agree that greatness is the end result of using said talent for the good of the people, number one is said as a cold fact, whereas number two is said with a sense of longing or of sacrifice.

So, if you have a talent that the world needs, employ it with all of your might. You will be serving your life purpose, possibly earning a living, and germinating the seeds of greatness all at the same time.

If all of us find something worthwhile that we are passionate about, it might pan out to be something that we were meant to do for the good of ourselves and mankind, but all to the glory of God.

The price you pay for forgoing your desires is nothing compared to the payday that you have coming in the immediate and eternal afterwhile.

"You can't beat God's giving, no matter how you try." (Doris Akers)

If you keep giving all that you have to a particular task then you become so good at that task that it becomes second nature to you. I mean, think about it. Take the easy task of walking. Though it is easy now, it was not always easy for you, was it? Most of us, if not all of us can summon up some of those toddler day memories of when we were first trying to learn to walk or when our children started to take their first toddling steps. But with practice and the passage of time, all of us have become proficient walkers able to hop, skip, and jump.

"A piece of cake," why did we become so proficient at walking? We gave it all we had, our best. And just like in the law of practice, each day's effort grew upon the efforts of the previois day. Before long, what had been so hard for us, had become our norm. That is such a simple thought to process, isn't it? Uhm hmm-m.

Well, living the Christian life can be likened to learning to walk. Here's how. If you practice the art of being kind on a daily basis, guess what you will become skilled at doing? Yes, being kind.

Now let's look at the flip side of that coin. If you practice being mean on a daily basis, guess what you will become skilled at doing? Exactly, being mean. **Whatever you practice on a daily basis is what you will become skilled at doing.** You can become good at being kind for the Master or you can become skilled in doing your best for jealousy, envy, being mean, etc., which glorifies the adversary. Which thing will afford you peace in eternity?

If you keep trying to
Do the best that you can do
You will find that the best of the best
Will spring forth from you.

Building upon the best that
Is today yours to give
Will manifest itself in greater ways
Than you ever thought could live
Inside of the body that you know of as yours
For you will become a master of the best, that
Each day, raises the personal bar of best-manifest.

****

Service Oriented

I spent the better part of
My life serving people
Fifteen years in Special Education
Fifteen years in the regular classroom
Trying to educate the youth of our nation
Beginning with the lessons in a book
And ending in showing them all
That they could bloom
As aromatic flowers in this garden
In which we have all been planted
By becoming successful in all that they undertook.

Coupled with working as a teacher
I worked forty-seven years as a help-meet
To my husband, who is a preacher.

No matter what congregation we went to
We tried to teach and show love so that the glory
Of God always came shining through.

Now, I am working full-time on my writing
Trying to tell the world that serving
My God is not boring, but exciting.

I have been allowed to build a legacy
And am writing a good bit of it down
So that you can read my story and hear my voice
As I try to pen words that are inspiring and sound.

Being service oriented is what the Lord desires
Because He told us so in John 13:15-17
And trying to lead a life that is pleasing to Him

Lift Up Your Voice

We serve mankind by not letting
Our Christian light go dim.

****

"If God be for us, then who can be against us?" *(Romans 8:31, KJV)*

That statement says it all for me. Let me explain, a little bit for you. All of my life, people have told me what I could and could not do, all according to their logic. You see, according to mankind's logic, one has to be popular, pretty, monied, live in the right neighborhood, etc., in order to be acclaimed by the masses and allowed to rise. But mankind's logic is not the same as the Lord's logic because God looks on the heart, whereas man looks on the outside. *(1 Samuel 16:7, KJV)* Furthermore, God is the master planner for all our lives, not man.

If the Lord has placed a certain thing in His plans for your life, then there is nothing that mankind can do to stop it. Absolutely nothing! Now, this does not mean that various folk have not tried to thwart His plans, but it does mean that GOD ALWAYS WINS!

A determined Christian often has to take this attitude: "I don't care what you think because the Lord God is omnipotent and is the planner of my life and of this entire world.

God is, and because God is, I will make it and have made it no matter what the world thinks or has thought."

We are in the Construction Business

Just a couple of things to grab your attention with reference to building. Webster defines building as an edifice (noun) or the act of constructing something (verb). Each day that we live, we are working on the building of something.

1. We are supplying, by our prayers, deeds, and words, building material for our home after this time side of life. Yes, we are in the construction business, indeed. John 14:3; Hebrew 11:6; Matthew 25:41. The way we live here determines the type of dwelling place that we will have on the eternal side of life.

2. We are constructing something that will be here long after we are gone. Yes, we are building a legacy one act at a time. It can impact our families, our communities, and our world in a positive or negative way. We can be like Lois and Eunice or like Jezebel. The choice is ours. Just remember that whatever you practice is what you will become best at.

Since we know that we are building day by day, what manner of builders ought we to be? Yep, we are building:

- For the here and now
- For a-while-later here on earth
- For all eternity

Working on Becoming a Master Builder
When you think about how the *here and now*
Impacts all of life, for times unseen
It makes you think and rethink some
Of the decisions that you have made
Or will have to make and you take on
A heavier load than than you here-to-fore had to bear
And you watch what you do and have a care
Because building is going on now, in the timed future
In the city that is being built up there.

****

What manner of builders ought we to be?

I Care Not

There is more that I can do, need to do and must do. This means that I must work on my habits by accentuating and escalating the positive ones and eradicating and diminishing the negative ones.

Another Day Closer

Another day closer
To my journey's end
Yet, even then I know
That I finish to begin.

Wisdom

I wrote this poem because of another phone call that I received. The lady said that she just had to hear my voice. That startled me for a second and I played it off and asked her how she was doing.

That is when she told me that there was just something about hearing my voice that made her feel better. She said that she needed her wisdom. Oka-ay. (gulp)

That floored me let me tell you. That was the second such phone call that I had received within as many weeks. I don't know why it should floor me but it did. I mean, I seem to have that effect on people. They seem to like to talk to me and to tell me their problems. I listen and then try to tell them some things to try to alleviate the problem. I also use soft and soothing words of understanding while I am talking to them.

In the paragraph above, I said that I should not be surprised about people's reaching out to me because that seems to happen in whatever sphere I am placed to work.

1. *When I taught school, the children gravitated to me with their problems and I was not even the guidance counselor.*
2. *At the congregation where my husband was minister for 26 years, quite a few of the sisters gravitated to me with their problems.*
3. And, it seems, that even now, when I am retired, people are still drawn to me.
4. You know how I sum that up? I say that it is a gift that He gave me to help keep people encouraged in their walk for Him. And I don't mind telling you that I take this job seriously.

I asked for wisdom every day as a child and the Lord God gifted me with some and I will use it for Him as long as I draw breath and can form coherent thought because a gift from God is not to be taken lightly.

1. What gift(s) have you been blessed with?
2. Do you use it for Him? Is the world aware of your gift? If not, why not?

Who Is She

Somebody said, "Who is she?" Those words may be uttered about a new person in a school, church, town, etc. Nobody knows anything about the newcomer until he or she does something to distinguish themselves.

That is the way we are when we first become Christians in that we have a clean slate. All past sins have been washed away. Then it becomes our task to write upon our clean slates by our actions from that point on.

So, when I go to a new place to live or just to visit, I want to leave an indelible impression upon the people that I meet. I want them to know that I know and love the Lord. I want to leave them lighter from having come into contact with me. I want to leave the essence of my journey with them in the form of a fire that cannot be quenched.

I want them to say, "I don't know who she is but one thing I do know is that she is not afraid to speak for God and tell about how He is a waymaker. I want them to say, "She is one of the redeemed."

> Let it be said when our day is done
> That we were willing to be one
> Who waved the banner of Christ
> By all that we said and did
> Until victory, at last, was won.
> ********

Case in Point

Yesterday, my husband took me to Patti's for dinner since it was the occasion of our 45th wedding anniversary. When you have reached this juncture in life, a good meal in a nice restaurant is all that is expected or required. Such was my state of contentment yesterday as I ate my meal with relish. My husband had already let the waiter and waitress and the diners around us know that it was our anniversary. About halfway through the meal, my husband stood up and said, "Excuse me, excuse me. Could I have your attention for a couple of seconds?" Everybody stopped talking and eating and turned expectant eyes upon him. He said, "If I don't do this, I will have to hear all about it when I get back to the car, so I am going to do this."

By this time, my head was hanging so low that my chin was practically resting on my chest. So you know how I was feeling as I wondered what inappropriate thing he was going to say now. I thought to myself, "You have already told them about the anniversary and received congratulations from them, what more can you say now? This is going to be a hot mess and I am stuck right here in the middle of it!"

I could feel every eyeball in the place on my bowed head with its hot little face. Then he said, "I just want you to know that this woman that you are eating with is an author and she has published five books."

My head shot up off my chest and, though my face was still warm, it no longer bore the look of shame that had been there seconds before. People started congratulating me and asking what types of books I had published. My husband said, "Stand up and tell them about your books, Alma."

I stood up and told about the five books that I had written. I spent the most time on my then latest, **Chopping My Row**. As I was talking about the book, people started nodding their heads and verbally agreeing with what I was saying. Then my husband told me that was enough because the people needed to finish their meals. I thanked them and sat back down promptly.

At the end of the meal, I went to the table behind me and asked if I might leave my card with them. They replied in the affirmative and we had some general laughing conversation and sharing time. I went to all the tables around us because they, too had been in the congratulatory words concerning the anniversary and the books.

Each table conversed with me as I was giving them my card. Some people teared up and others thanked me for my words. One woman yelled out, before I could get to her table, "Now where did you say that we could get that book?" I told her and I saw several others scrambling for pens to write on the cards that I had given them.

All in all, an enjoyable time and I only went there to det dinner, But I left the diners that we ate with feeling elated and myself feeling the same.

"Now, why did I take the time to tell you about my dining experience," some of you might be wondering. I told you about it because I wanted to say that we are in the spotlight, whether we realize or not. We just never know when it is going to be turned fully on us. So, let's be aware of that and be caught allowing the glory of God to be shining when the spotlight does get trained upon us.

And remember, always be prepared to speak about the justice, righteousness and lovingkindness of the Lord. As I've told you before, He delights in that. (Jeremiah 9:24)

My Gift
God sent me to earth with a valuable gift
The ability to dream and to give folks' spirits a lift
Many people have had a go at me
And try though they might
The Lord did not allow this intrinsic gift
To be removed from my embattled sight.

So
If I helped you once or many times, down through the years
Perhaps by making you laugh or by wiping your tears
It was my appointed duty to do so
And it is with joy that I see that you
Are remaining steady as you go.
If
If you have been and are one of the angels sent
To cross my path or stay a while to keep me
Focused and shored up regarding my life's intent
To you, I say, "Bless you and thank you and I
Make mention of you often in my talks with the God of eternity.

When
Each time that you run across me
Working on my dreams of motivating humanity
My stepping on is what you will see
As I look to the hills toward my destiny.
****

"The dream you gave me, Lord, I tried to keep," is what I say to my Lord, ere I go to sleep.

Poetry Offerings for Lesson 7

The Mark of Endurance

An old soldier wearily made his way home
With victory in his scarred grasp
His body marred by blows inflicted
While upon life's battlefield
His visage carved into a winning smile
That had carried him through mile after mile
Of enemy assault in his quest to show that
The love He felt for Jesus was real.

Somebody asked him how he could still
Smile after all that he had been through
He replied, "It's easy enough if you remember
To pray, bearing in mind that He hears, answers and sustains you.

Just keep traveling the way that you are and one day you will be
The battle hardened soldier that you see in me
And one day you will walk with a soldier's assurance
Carrying the sign of working for the Savior,
The mark of Christian endurance."

The Glory of God in You

Somebody said to me
"Alma, you are so good
At what you do.
You have helped me weather
The storm I was going through.
You made me feel much better
By what you had to say

I was down in the dumps
Before I talked to you
But now I feel revived and refreshed
Because of your doing what you do."
I replied, "Thank you, but it is not me that is
Good at what you see me do
It is just the glory of God shining through."

****

I got the chance to skip
After I had learned to walk
And before then, crawl
I got the chance to work
After I had learned to play
I got the chance to experience
Life to its fullest, y'all
But you know what I am proud of most of all
I got the chance to serve the Lord, my GOD in the plan
That HE had written before I was born
As a teacher, minister's wife and writer
To help place encouragement in the lives of man.

Lift Up Your Voice

Discussion Questions

1. Will all Christians suffer persecution?

_____

_____

_____

_____

2. According to Philippians 2:15, what is the duty of Christians to the world?

_____

_____

_____

_____

3. How is 1 Peter 5:7 a comfort to troubled Christians?

_____

_____

_____

_____

4. Why should Christians be careful about what they do?
(Matthew 5:16, KJV)

_____

_____

_____

_____

5. How can a storm be a blessing to you? (Psalm 107, KJV)

_____

_____

_____

_____

6. Are we in control of our own lives? *(Acts 17:28, KJV)*

_____

_____

_____

_____

What Do You Think?

1. How can you become skilled at being kind?

_____

_____

_____

_____

For Further Reading
Psalm 139:13-16

This Moment in Time
What I do for you at any given moment in time
Is really no biggie at all
Because wrapped up in what I do
Is the love that Jesus has for me, and for you
I just ask that you be the hand that lifts another from a fall
And pass the love along
And by doing so, help somebody else to be strong.

Lesson 8:

Love Makes Me Do It

Scripture: John 3:16; Matthew 22:29; Ephesians 6:18; 1 Thessalonians 3:12-13

Aim: TO BE MINDFUL OF THE FACT love should be the motivating factor for everything that we do. TO KNOW THAT we should pray for others as we serve God.

Song: It's in My Heart to Serve the Lord

I Love You

The words, "I love you," elicit a warm response from most people. To a child, it might mean, "I care about you and will take care of you until you are an adult." To someone else, it might mean, "Your welfare is important to me." Still, to someone else, it might mean, "You are cherished and adored for what you have done or for who you are." There are many more connotations that people put with the words, "I love you."

But to me, those words make me think of the Trinity: God, the Father, Jesus, the Son, and the Holy Spirit. I think of God because He showed His love by the sacrifice of His only begotten Son to save a sinful world. I think of Jesus because He laid down His life to save me because He loved His Father and loved me because His Father loved me. I think of the Holy Spirit because He works tirelessly with me at the request of the Lord.

In the same vein, but not to the same magnitude, I love you, dear reader. Why? I love you because it is commanded by God and because I love Him. I don't know how to show my love fully to Him, but I can try to show it by the service I perform for Him. Part of that service is to, 1. love you, since you are precious to Him and 2. to love myself. (Matthew 22:29, KJV)

Did you know that I write because of the love that I have for God and subsequently, you? Well, I do. You see, if I needed to hear some encouraging words, I would read my Bible, sing encouraging songs to myself, write in my journal, etc.

But for you, just in case there are those among you who need encouraging words, and who doesn't from time to time, I do a daily blog and write inspirational books.

Yes, my writing is a part of my service to God. I am helping to keep His people from growing so weary that they faint in the tasks that they have been given to do. (Isaiah 50:4, KJV) Yep, you might say that I am one of the Lord's mouthpieces and proud of it.

Yes, and as syrupy as my writing is sometimes, there are those among us that have become so embittered that it takes a coating of syrupy words to soften the hard shell with which they have knowingly or unknowingly encased themselves.

And now you know why I have this drive to write – love.

Love Makes Me Want to Cause God to Smile

Do you believe in prayer? I mean really believe? You do? Good! Now for the next question, do you love your fellowman? Really love him? Uhm-hmm, well here is a quick thought. How often do you pray for your fellowman? As often as you pray for your family? Uhm hmm.

No, folks do not pray for their fellowman as often as they do for their family. But you know, quite a few folks pray morning and night for their fellowman. That is admirable.

Do you remember the boys and coach in Thailand that were trapped in a cave? Uhm-hmm, caring people prayed for their rescue several times a day. I know I did! Wasn't it a thrilling relief when they all were rescued?

Here is another hypothetical question for you. How do you think that God felt with so many prayers coming up from all over the globe for those boys? Do you think that it made Him smile? We don't know but I can imagine that it did.

Let's make God smile some more. When you go to worship, make it a point to really concentrate during prayer time and pray for your fellowman the world over. If all of you who read this book will do that, we can cause God to smile. That, my friend, is an awesome thing to do. You might mention in your prayer that this was suggested by a book you read today.

You might ask, "Why mention that?" Well, to my way of thinking, we know that God knows everything. But when He sees that you read a book that was suggesting prayer for your fellowman in worship, and that you actually followed through with it, that fact will cause Him to smile more.

I think the fact that, because of love for your fellowman, you followed through with a suggestion from a book, will go a long way toward endearing you and your future prayers to Him, should trouble arise in your life.

Then too, the fact that there are those among His creation, who hold Him dear and near just might make Him brag on you. Your fellowman does include your preacher and your President, you know. Well! They need prayers being sent up for them, too.

Serving in Love Despite the Surprise

I received two surprises yesterday and here is how they came about.

Recently we celebrated the 43rd anniversary of my home congregation located in Martin, Tennessee. There were people there from out of town who were members before life caused them to relocate. It was good to see all. God is good.

As far as the title of this piece, I was asked to sing a song yesterday and I managed to hide my surprise and was not much nervous at all. I took myself on up front, made eye contact with my audience and connected my heart to theirs through song.

I have always wanted to sing, and people have told me often enough that I can sing, but it didn't settle into me until yesterday when I had to sing a song on the spur of the moment and didn't have the words written down. And, as I mentioned above, there was very little nervousness.

What exactly were my two surprises, you ask? Well, as a husband and wife team, my husband and I have an agreement that he will never ask me to sing or do anything in public before he has forewarned me. He totally ignored that rule yesterday, first surprise. And my second surprise was that I was not nervous much at all about having to sing without having my song written down. Y'all, usually I am so nervous that I will forget the words if I do not have them written down. Yes, I enjoyed my two little surprises.

And no, I am not the best singer around, but the Lord didn't say that I had to "be" the best, He just said do my best. And that is what I attempt to do each day of my life.

Little Things Mean a Lot

I was reading a blog entry this morning, just by chance, and ran across a list of nice little things to do to help others. I was amazed by how many of the things on the list were things, owing to my mother's instruction, that I do on a regular basis, so I was inspired to create my own list:

1. "Give more hugs. Research has shown that hugging makes you healthier, so start giving more hugs.
2. Say please and thank you often. Never underestimate the power of a simple thank-you (something I have told you many times).
3. Speaking of thank-yous, send thank-you notes. Not just for your wedding gifts but for everything. Send thank you notes for people that, in doing their jobs, do a routine service for you. You know how it makes you feel when someone shows their appreciation to you. Well do the same for someone else.
4. Let pregnant and elderly people have your seat on the bus or train. (a no-brainer)
5. Open doors. Hold the door open for someone carrying a bunch of groceries or a suitcase.

6. Empty the dishwasher. Why not be a better roommate?
7. Don't leave your dirty dishes in the sink. Put them in the dishwasher you just emptied.
8. Pick up after yourself. If you're at a restaurant or café that doesn't have a busser, put your dirty dishes in the designated area. Throw away your trash.
9. Don't leave your shopping cart in the middle of the parking lot. Put it in the corral with the rest of the carts.
10. Give away the books you've read. Go through your bookshelves. Pull out any books you no longer want and donate them to a local library. (If they gave you information and or joy then share that pleasure with someone else.)
11. When driving through a bridge toll or drive-in restaurant or coffee shop, pay for the car behind you.
12. Do what you say you're going to do. Always keep your word.
13. Respond to emails, texts, and phone calls. Don't ignore your friends and family.
14. When someone says hello, say hi back. It's just plain rude not to.
15. Let people through in traffic. When people cut you off, don't flip them off. Let it go.
16. Be an active and thoughtful listener. When you ask people how they are, listen intently to their response.
17. Leave a generous tip to someone who has done a good job.
18. Give more compliments. A simple "I love your dress" can go a long way.
19. Call your parents every day because one day they may be where you cannot reach them.
20. Let someone who is in a hurry go ahead of you at the checkout line.
21. Make someone else's bed. Your roommate, sibling, or

spouse will love you for it. It shows that you can be considerate.

22. Smile at strangers.
23. Buy a sandwich for the homeless person in front of the grocery store.
24. Take the garbage out.
25. Put change in a meter that's about to expire.
26. Praise someone who is doing an amazing job.
27. Pay attention to your children. Put down your phone and give them your undivided attention.
28. Volunteer.
29. Interact with the people you encounter every day. Talk to the guys who work at the corner store. Develop a friendly relationship with the lady who makes your coffee just how you like it.
30. Forget about a debt that someone owes you. Ask the person who was supposed to pay you back to do the same to someone else in the future.
31. Stop complaining. Your positivity will encourage other people to do the same.
32. Be tolerant and flexible. Stick up for someone being treated wrongly.
33. Do a loved one's laundry.
34. Be a positive impact rather than a negative one. A kind person is authentic and aware of how their actions can affect people. *'What Are the Benefits of Hugging,' healthline.com*

In essence, practice being kind. The world will be a better place because of it. *(Colossians 3:12, KJV)*

Here is a poem that I have written for your pleasure and thought today:

When I write a poem for you
In hopes of brightening your day
I am practicing love by giving
A part of myself away
In hopes that you will feel pleasant enough
To share a kindness with another along the way.

You Are Special ... If

Up the mountain and through the valley I go
Undeterred because I am special, don't you know?
Though assaulted by enemies time and time again
I keep walking by faith because Jesus is my friend.
He loves me and shows me that He does by saying of me,
"She is mine."
I tell you, folks, there is no better friend that anyone could find.

****

I'm special, you know why
Because the Father's love dwells within me
And He has given me gifts to share with all humanity.
You are special, too
Why, because there is also a loving gift(s)
Summarily placed inside of you.

You may have a tender ear
Coupled with a loving heart
Or you may be gifted with the
Power of persuasive speech

It really does not matter
What the gift is that you possess
Just use that spark within you
To brighten somebody's day
And help them find their own path
As they travel on their way.

Just think about that the next time that you have the opportunity to make somebody happy or to make them sad. And choose the higher road by calling on the love that He has placed within you to brighten another's life. You can leave that person thinking that they were so lucky to run into you on that particular day. And you can think to yourself and say to them as well, "It's not luck, it's love – the love of God, that is."

Love Makes Me Show Some Love

Today when I awoke, I awoke with a feeling of extra love and gratitude. Because I am so grateful for God's goodness in my life, oftentimes I will do something kind for someone. As you know, sometimes I prepare a meal for a bachelor minister who has been on the battlefield a long time.

Well, he recently got out of the hospital, and I know that nothing makes you feel more special than having a home cooked dish delivered to your door. So, today I made one of his favorite desserts, banana pudding. I sent my husband over with the dish and fried chicken as well. He already had his vegetables, so my food was right on time.

When I lie down to sleep tonight, I can think that I made someone happy today other than my family, you know? All of us have things that we can do to help to lighten someone's load or brighten someone's day.

Here's his banana pudding. Have a bite.

Yes, I did make one to keep at home, as well. Be blessed.

Another Way of Showing My Love
Go to worship service and give God some glory
Because His giving us His best love is an age-old story.

My Lot

It has fallen my lot to touch several lives in significant ways. I often wondered why I was saved, but I don't wonder anymore.

Read the poem below to garner my meaning.

Saved

One day several decades ago
At an apartment building located
At 1442 N. Stonewall St.
Down in Memphis, Tennessee
Zip Code 38107
Lived a little eight-year-old girl
Who should have, that day, died and gone to heaven
But God would not let it be
Though she broke the laws of nature
When she reached into her pocket
Pulled out a safety pin and
Stuck it into a wall socket!

Yes, reader, I realize that without God's lovingkindness
My life would no longer be
Because I would have already
Finished my walk on this earth
And arrived at the place of my eternal destiny.

I began to be aware of God's favor that day and I have finally
understood that it is not about me and what I understand or what I
think should be, but about doing the will of the Creator. I just do
what good falls to my hand to do in spreading sunshine and hope
in every place that I live, work or reside. If I do that then I will be
in the ballpark of my life goal.

Do what good that is in your hand to do
Because you never know why a
Particular task was parceled out to you.

Love Makes Me Go the Extra Mile - A Team of Superstars

In sports, there are situations that come about that result in a team of superstars. It could come about because of some family moving in because of a job loss in one area, or moving to be closer to an ailing relative, etc. Nevertheless, whatever the reason is for the move, it ends in the compilation of a team that thinks as a cohesive unit in order to get a job done.

This does not apply to sports only, but to any sphere in life. It could be a corporate team, a church team, a neighborhood team, etc. It usually ends up being people that share like values or like passions for a cause.

To be known for caring is a great attribute. To be known for being organized is laudable, as well. To be known for being a "take charge person" can be laudable nomenclature, too. And when you have a group that finds themselves pushed together by chance with all of the characteristics described in the beginning sentence of this paragraph, that is something. You have a team of superstars!

Imagine the good that such a team can do in the work of the Lord. Such a team has been brought to my attention. Each person does whatever is at hand to get a particular job done. The team builds upon each other's strength and fills out any weak spots. Much like a well-played sports event, the job at hand gets done in finesse of style. If you can find yourself such a group, then the tasks that you undertake will get done so much faster. I know because I have found such a team. Only God!

Ernestine, Shirley, and Stacey – Superstars! Ladies, take a bow!

Love Makes Me Brave the Snow

A bit of snow and ice fell in our area last night. Though they do not attend the same congregation, the ladies that make up the team of superstars mentioned above brave the snowy weather in their various towns to attend worship so that they can be positive examples for others, as we all should strive to be. Inclement weather like this always reminds me of that scripture that says, "Where two or three are gathered in my name, there I will be in the midst." (Matthew 18:20, KJV) This type of weather in the south cuts church attendance down to a minimum.

Be that as it may, the *two or three* of us that gather are important enough to Jesus for Him to be in our midst. I am glad about that. Just think the Potentate of potentates, meeting with us. That means that we are somebody to Jesus!

Well, must go. I have a meeting with the Potentate!

It is an icy snow snowy day in the area where I live
Yet, I am going to tuck into my snow gear
And attend worship service so that I
Can open my mouth and praises to Jesus give.

I aim to be one of the two or three
Present when the Lord comes in the air
And I aim to be in attendance whether
The weather is foul or fair
Because this somebody is waiting for Jesus
Who has a prepared place in heaven
For the day that I arrive there.

****

Love Makes Me Pray for You

My goal in life is to encourage, uplift, listen to, and be a positive example for my fellowman. This is done in love because love is what is commanded by God.

In keeping with that command, I wanted to let you know that I lifted you up in prayer this morning. Why? I did it because I prayed for myself, and as we are to love others as we love ourselves, I prayed for you, too.

Now, I want you to pray for yourself and others. As a matter of fact, make it a habit of praying for others in the world daily. If you want peace in our world, lend your voice to the ones that are praying for it. Whatever your concern is, pray about it. And don't stop. Do it on a continual basis. Everyday.

"The effectual fervent prayer of the righteous availeth much." (James 5:16, KJV)

"...draw near with confidence to the throne of grace, that we may receive mercy and find grace to help in time of need." (Hebrews 4:16, KJV)

Let's link our thoughts together as we send up prayers to the Lord for the betterment of mankind and our world. Who knows, perhaps they (your and my prayers) will meet each other at our Father's throne, just as you and I will one of these days.

In Keeping

Be blessed and remember, "God loves you, and I do, too."

Don't you feel special just knowing there are people out there who pray for you just because you are a part of mankind that draws breath? Yes, precious, even you... That is what is so sweet about it. He did not say that you had to deserve love. He said to love you and so I do. Yep, sure do, sweetie. You see, it's like this, none of us deserve it or are worthy, but He loves us anyway, and so, we do you. It's that simple!

Case in Point

When I was teaching school, I always looked for the stars in my pupils' eyes when they first entered my classroom. I looked for those stars midyear and again at the end of the year. It was always heartwarming to see that despite the rigorous work schedule, the stars remained as bright as ever in the ones who came to me with stars. But along with them, stars shone in eyes that had previously been jaded or dulled before they came to my class for social studies. The eyes that shone with a renewed love for learning are the ones that kept me going year after year.

As a Christian, when I can shore up someone's faith and renew hope where hope has died, that is the thing that keeps me going day after day. You see, if I can do that then I know that I will hear my Father say, "Well done." It is the hope of hearing those words that keeps me *stepping on*. I have a reward that I am working for, folks. It's as simple as that.

Think About It

There is a place that is being prepared for me where the "wicked will cease from troubling and the weary shall be at rest."

Told You I Would Go
I told You I would go
And that's just what I did

I have been high and I have been low
But it did not matter because
I told You I would go.

I gave my heart to the Lord when I was just a child. I didn't know the path that He would place me on just like I don't know where my path will lead me today. But one thing I can tell you is that when you continue to give your all to the Lord, He will remember who you are in your good times as well as in your rough times.

Another Season

Another season has arrived
This one with leaves ablaze
So blessed, so blessed to have
Seen a plethora of days
And to think, to think
God kept me through
All of my ways.
Going to the church house
This morning to confess
That I indeed am happy and blessed.

So, if you can see the colors of fall
You have been blessed, too
Go to worship and show your neighbor
That you thank Him for all He allows you to do
Just displaying your gratitude for your fellowman
Is just one of the ways that you can say to God
"Thank You, Lord, for allowing me to be able
To say, 'I can.'"

The Valley of the Crossroads

Up from the valley of the crossroads
I arose on this worship day
To realize once again that God had
Given me the power to stick and stay
Faithful to Him throughout the battle fray.

Sunday promises to be a full day of worship for me. I will attend morning worship and approach my Father's throne in reverence and in awe. I will approach His throne in thanksgiving and in humbleness. I am going to close my eyes and sing to my Father for His goodness in being my Shepherd and in keeping the wolves at bay. I am going to pray earnestly for the church all over the world and for mankind in general.

When I leave morning worship, it will be to journey to another congregation to fellowship with them and take my food offering to share as well. After that, I will journey back and worship with another congregation for the night service.

In all of my journeying today, I will try to spread some love along the way. I will have the opportunity to touch lives in moments in time that have never been before and never will again because once a moment is gone, it cannot be recaptured. Precious are the minutes that we are allowed to live in this world and with the passage of time, I realize that fact more and more.

It is my aim to lift someone from the valley of the crossroads and lead them gently to the Savior's loving arms. How can I do this? I can do so by living a life that says:

Crossroads
"Hello, how are you today
Crossroads come and crossroads go
But you are safe in His arms, of Jesus you know
And never forget that the battle my dear
Is always fiercest when victory is near
Just saying in passing as I go on my way.

You see, I have determined within my soul
To serve my Lord by serving you
Yes, fellowman, that is my goal.

And if in my service I have to cry
I arm myself with the knowledge that
Jesus will wipe every tear-stained eye
And I will not have to cry anymore
When I get home to that other shore.

Having said that, you have a good day
And use/store these words in the memory of your heart
Against the time when the valley of
The crossroads blocks your way."

There are some people who seem to thrive on being negative and not being nice. Here is a quick story.

Case in point

Yesterday I was in the grocery store and a gentleman came up to the counter where I was having some meat cut. He came up to the lady on the other end of the counter and told her something about his bucket of chicken not containing by weight what it should have, I was taken aback by his general demeanor and rudeness.

He told the lady waiting on him that it was a good thing that there are honest people in the world because they keep the rest of us honest. And mind you, he did not say this with a smile.

Well, his statement riled the lady who was waiting on him and the lady who was waiting on me, too. I looked at the one who was waiting on me and I started talking about what a nice time of year it was. She responded, "Yes, it is. I love Fall!" I could see that she was trying not to be upset by the rude man's comments, but was losing the battle.

Then I piped up with, "You know, God is so good to us. Now you take the seasons. He has put something breathtaking in each season. We just finished talking about the fall leaves, and in the winter there is the snow. And you know that is beautiful. Have you ever taken the time and listened to the snow? Have you ever heard those huge flakes hitting the ground loud enough that you can hear them when they land?"

Y'all, I could see that my ploy was working. Then I talked about the joy that we feel when we see that first Spring flower. She readily agreed with me. And then I mentioned the pretty green grass of summer. Then I made her feel extra loved when I said, "You know how when you are working outside and cannot go in and it is so hot that you wish to yourself that the Lord would send a breeze? And then you get that nice cooling breeze. What a joy and what a blessing!

I had her by then. She had stopped glaring at the rude gentleman and was smiling and talking to me. Now, y'all know me. When I saw that I had her fully engaged in the conversation, I sweetly and innocently drove home a sweet spot for her to remember for the rest of the day.

I told her that one day about a week or so ago, I was reading my Bible and I saw where it said that the Lord kept the wind in His storehouses, His treasuries. I said that means that when we get that cooling breeze, that the Lord has sent us that cooling breeze just because He loves mankind. Then I told her, "And that's why I can keep smiling in difficult situations, you know?"

She said yes she did know and that she read her Bible, too. But sometimes when people are rude when you are already overworked, it gets hard. That's when I told her, "Yes, that's true, but you know. Just knowing that He has put things in all of the seasons because He wants us to be happy and when I think about the wind being sent all of the way from heaven, I get stirred up with joy. And that is why I will not allow anybody to steal my joy that the Lord sent to me."
She looked at me and gave me the biggest smile and then she said, You are right and thank you for talking to me. She was still smiling when I left the counter.

My Point

Take the time to show a little loving kindness because you never know who is having a bad day. Furthermore, how do you think Jesus looked when He saw that I defused the situation and spread some joy? Exactly!

> You may meet all kinds of folk on any given day
> So make sure that you give then positive feedback
> And send them merrily on their way
> Equipped to better deal with the "some people"
> No matter what they do or say.

What Would You Think

What would you think if the emergency response person, the fireman, the taxi driver, the doctor, etc. refused to come out to work because of rain or a storm? You would be horrified and indignant, and rightly so. Yet so often, we as Christians, allow the Lord's work to be short-changed or nonexistent when we have *rain or storms* in our lives. That should not be the case. We need to realize that our lives are not all about us, but rather about living to influence others to love the Lord as we do. If I love Him, I am going to do what I can to help save souls. *(Jude 23, KJV)* Luke 15:7 tells us that "There is joy in Heaven over a sinner that repents."

There is nothing more valuable in this world of ours than souls. With that being the case, we must work for the Lord, even in the event of storms or rain in our lives. Our work must continue in the rain and storms. It is just that important! And remember, I told you in Lessons Three and Seven that we influence people to love and trust God or not by our actions.

Somebody might say, "Well, since He sees that I am out here working for Him, He ought to make the rain come later, or the storms completely go away or never arise in the first place." Tsk, tsk, tsk! Remember the scripture that said, "All who live godly shall suffer persecution." *(2 Timothy 3:12, KJV)*

Lessons and Strength
There is something in the rain
There is a good reason for all my pain.

Repentantly Working

Doing My Job
Repentantly working
Diligently watching
Patiently waiting
As I encourage my fellowman
To get ready for Jesus to come again.

Standing Alone

Standing Alone
Sometimes in life, we are forced to take a stand
It may be that we feel strongly enough about a principle
To not worry about being popular with our fellowman.

During my tenure on this earth, my skin
Color has oftentimes set me apart
But be that as it may, no one but God and me can determine
The impact that my tenure here can or will have
Or how bright or high my star will shine or rise
Because the possibilities were ordained before my start.

So, if I end up standing alone and standing out
I'll make sure that the principle I become known for
Depicts the godly beliefs that I am all about.

****

I am here
I see
Yet, I am persevering
Because the God of Heaven
Sustains and guides me
And, as I have said before,

The influence of my life
Is up to God, ultimately.

Bottom line is that it doesn't matter
What you do, say, or write about me
Because when I am gone my deeds will
Be judged by Jesus, the Prince of eternity.

Sure, I have problems like everybody else, but I am determined to not allow misery to be comfortable in my company. So, I talk to the Lord and give Him my cares. And then I have the courage to stand up, stand out and when I have to, stand alone, all done by the grace of God, I know.

———————————

Poetry Offerings for Lesson 8

(I make no apologies for what I am in my walk with Him, though it has caused me to be ridiculed and ostracized from time to time. But you know, it matters not because I am not my own. However, I do tend to be a bit wayward at times. What does He do when I am wayward? Like the loving Father that He is, He tightens my reins and pulls me right back to Him, where I belong. Thus saving me from myself.

He really is awesome, wonderful, and full of love *and I owe Him so much. And that is why I offer this poetic tribute of praise to Him this day.)*

Doing Your Job

When you go to your job
By which you make your living
Things are not always pleasant and
Do not always go your way
But you punch that clock regardless
Because you need to earn your pay.

Well just as crucial to you is the
Job that you must do for your soul
Because "Work well- Great pay"
Is what you have been promised
On that great getting up day.

Yes, on the one hand, you work for your living
And on the other hand you work for your destiny
Oh, how well laid and interlaced is this existence
That we know of as humanity.

God's Love

I ran across a scripture the other day that made me pause. "Are they not all ministering spirits, sent forth to do service for the sake of them that shall inherit salvation?" (Hebrews 1:14, ASV)

I did a little reference on it and the poem below is the result.

God's Love

God's love surrounds us in ways we
Do not often think about
But His love is with us nonetheless
In the "ministering spirits that be."

I'm thankful for His ministrations
On my behalf and often tell Him so
In fact, I speak my thanks and praise
To all who listen, everywhere I go.

Let It Be About Love

If I say that I love you
You do not have to wonder
If that is true
For I shower you with
Tender acts that say,
"Sister Alma cares about you."

You show love
You show hate
Cold indifference is

A clandestine form of hurt or hate
Which emotion have
You shown of late?

Going to Worship
Taking with me to worship
Each request asked of me
For each person
Who toils in the Lord's way
Gonna lay it all at Jesus' feet
When I, with the other saints
In prayerful contemplation meet.

Forward I Go

Jeremiah 29:11 has let me know
That You have already made plans
For me and armed with that
Knowledge, it is forward that I go.

I see in nature when I look around
That you never leave situations to chance
For Your meticulous preparation
Can be seen throughout all creation
You plan things down to minute details
And because of that fact, I get assurance
When I think of the plans You have made for me
And armed with the knowledge of Your love
I walk on with surety.

When I think about the fact that Your
Omnipotent hands fashioned me in my work

In the way that You wanted me to chop my row
I get renewed vigor and tenacity
No matter what is thrown at me by my foe
And it is with relish that I tell the world
My God loves you and me and this is a
Fact that I know
(Chopping My Row, p. 8)

I put my heart into the things that I pen for you, fellowman,
because I want to travel to various places within your soul
leaving healing touches where needed as we learn and discover
together the marvelous love that He has for you and me.

I try to remember what first I felt in a given moment of epiphany
and then I convey that awe, excitement and exuberance to you. I
try to lead you on my sensory journey and deposit you with grace
at the Lord's feet. In keeping with that, here is a poem for you
today:

Unrealistically Optimistic
That is what they termed me
They said that I couldn't go to college
Because my family had no connections and no money
It was just not possible, you see
But I was optimistic because
I knew the God Who dwells in me.

They said I would never get a
Regular classroom in said county, Tennessee
Because I was Black and from out of town
It was just not possible, you see
But I was optimistic because
I knew the God that dwells in me.

Even today when I am told
You can't do this and you cannot do that
It's just not possible, you see
I just look at them with a serene smile
For I know the God Who dwells in me!

The Greatest Love of All
The love of God is the greatest love of all
He gave His Son's life to save us from our fall
And He is ever ready to heed our bleating call
How blessed we are to know that we are recipients of
The greatest love of all.

**Hatred begets hatred and kindness does the same.
So, as we live this day, this life,
Let's sow love in Jesus' name.**

One Last Time

There is one last thing I need to discuss with you concerning
love. I am sure that you have discussed, at some point, your
preferences should you leave this life, but there are some little
things that fall through the cracks.

If you love your family, there is a way that you can make things a
bit easier for the ones that have to take care of your funeral.
While death is not a pleasant topic, it is a part of life.

A few years ago, I had to help a friend write an obituary for their
parent. Here's the thing. The ones who prepare your obituary
may not know:

- where you were born
- the school you graduated from
- the full name and birthdate of your parents (especially if estranged)
- any special persons you want to be mentioned in your obituary, etc.

These are all things that you take for granted until the time comes when you need such information.

Case in Point

When I lost my Momma, I was in such a fog that it was hard to function. I did everything from being in a lethargic stupor to crying uncontrollably. But my Momma, bless her sweet heart, knew that the preparations would fall on me and that I would be a basket case since I was the only girl and we had been like sisters. Here is what my Momma did to help me one last time:

1. Before she passed, she told me where to have her funeral and who to officiate. (That is pretty much a given, as most parents do that.) But she didn't stop there.
2. She left a detailed list of how she wanted each of her personal items disposed of including writing the names of people on the bottom of shoes that she wanted to have them. Things that she did not have a preference for who got them, she simply wrote girl – enjoy.
3. She tagged the dress and shoes that she wanted to be buried in, though we had discussed this many times. I think that she did that because she knew that I would be distraught, and she was correct.

Those things listed in the numbered account above served to

remind me of the caring individual that she was and I can tell you that that little touch of thoughtfulness reached through my grief and wrapped me in her arms one more time. She was thoughtful and considerate of others one last time (me).

In my mind, it was like I was feeling her love for me one more time because these were the last things she touched and she wrote little notes and tagged items especially for me. To me, it was like she was holding my hand as I tried to go through her things and decide what to do with which thing.

Of course, you know that I had to leave her house after only five minutes the first time because it was just too hard to do. But I carried the thought of the tags and notes that she had written for me and the next time, I was able to stay an hour, and so forth. I could hear her voice in my mind's eye, saying in the matter-of-fact way that she had, "This is just the way that it is and you can do this because I told you before, you are stronger than you think you are."

Y'all, I know that I am a Momma's baby, but those little things she did have carried me far, just as her words have colored my life so much that I have put her teachings all through the books I have authored, as well as my life.

So, make a will, list, etc., to help your family one last time. Your thoughtfulness will reach through their grief and wrap them in your arms one last time. The thoughtful *"hug"* from you will be remembered by them for the rest of their lives.

As I Said

This is not a popular nor comfortable topic but a necessary one, nonetheless.

I mean, Jesus left a testament of His love for man as a tool to help carry us through life and the apostles passed that Testament forward to us, today.

Be blessed and remember, God loves you and I do, too.

Discussion Questions

1. According to Matthew 22:29, how much love are we to show others?

_____

_____

_____

_____

2. Why is it important to show kindness? *(Col. 3:12, KJV)*

_____

_____

_____

_____

3. Are we to pray for others? *(James 5:16, KJV)*

_____

_____

_____

_____

4. If I am a Christian and say I love God, must I help to save souls? How?

_____

_____

_____

_____

5. How does Heaven feel over one sinner that repents?

_____

_____

_____

_____

What Do You Think

1. How do you think Jesus looks when He sees you diffuse a tense situation and spread joy instead?

_____

_____

_____

For Further Reading
Galatians 6:20; 1 Timothy 2:1-5; James 5:16, 19-20; Proverbs 11:30; Titus 2:7

When the Lord Has Singled You Out
When the Lord has singled you out
You cease to be like everybody else
So, stop fighting it
For God knows what He is about.

Lesson 9:

Ladies Day Speaker

Scripture: 1 Peter 4:10-11; Matthew 5:14-16; 1 Thessalonians 5:11; 1 Corinthians 1:10; Psalm 139:13-16

Aim: TO REALIZE THAT being a cohesive part of the church is pleasing to God. TO REALIZE THAT being all that we can be shows the Lord that we love Him and others. TO REALIZE THAT often in working for the Lord, we are given tasks that seem too difficult, but by the doing, we grow in our work for Him, all according to His plan.

Song: This Little Light of Mine

So you want to be a ladies' day speaker? Have you ever thought about it?

> At long last, I have learned to wait on His plan for my life
> Because He does things in His own good time
> And finds no need to hurry
> – After all, He is the Architect, Who
> Ushers in all things eternal and sublime.

Love into Words

I want to invite you to prayerfully think about what more you can do for God, Whom you love.

Case in Point

One day, I was asked to speak to a group of ladies at church for our upcoming ladies' day program. I didn't want to do it because I felt like I was not a speaker and would do an abysmal job. I didn't want to be laughed at about the miserable job that I knew I would do. But because I was the preacher's wife, I decided to do it.

One thing about being a preacher's wife, you get pushed into many areas that you are not used to and are not comfortable in, either. But I had promised to be a helpmeet for my husband, and as such, that meant taking on uncomfortable tasks at times.

What Did I Do

I panicked, and then I took my dilemma to God, and I told Him about what the ladies had asked me to do, and I told Him how scared I was. I asked Him to help me to do a good job. After that, I chose my topic and started doing some research and making some notes. I listened to some preacher's sermons, and if they said something that grabbed my attention, I jotted that down. One thing I can say about the ladies at the congregation where my husband was the minister at the time, they believed in preparing a year ahead of time for any of their ladies' days. And that was good because I had a whole year to get prepared.

Also, I looked for certain passages that jumped out at me as I was reading my Bible. It was amazing how often my daily Bible reading presented me with additional thoughts for my lesson. Before long, I had a hodgepodge of notes. I started reading them and lumping them together into categories where I thought they might fit. I used an outline like the following:

- Introduction
- First subtopic
- Second subtopic
- Third subtopic
- Conclusion

Using that format, I was able to prepare my lesson for the ladies. After I got the lesson polished on paper, I set about getting my presentation polished. How did I do that?

- I started practicing recording myself on my hand-held tape recorder.
- When I was satisfied with that, I started presenting my speech to myself in the mirror. *(Nowadays, there is technology where you can record yourself speaking in practice and play it back as you watch yourself. My, what a long way the Lord has allowed us to come technologically!)*
- I prepared visual aids in the form of PowerPoint or actual material things that could be used to further bring out my point. I was making my presentation to an audience of one.
- I timed myself doing the lesson and made sure that it was no more than 30 minutes, preferably 20 because you lose your audience if it is any longer.

Success
Doing the things mentioned above made me a polished speaker, with some acclaim. It was nothing for me to be asked to speak at various ladies' days in our area and some secular events.

Whenever I was asked, I always took it to God first and asked Him to guide me. After that, I worked as if everything depended on me. I have learned that if you give your all in preparation for doing something for Him, He will come through for you.

Bringing It Home

If you are working for the Lord and are serious about it, often you will have no choice in the things that you are asked to do. But rest assured that if you ask Him to, He will help you get the job done. Why? He does it because you are His child, whom He loves, and you are putting yourself on the line for Him.

So, whatever you do for Him, do it in love. *(Luke 10:27, KJV)* Love will drive you to do things that you never thought that you could or would. What is your ministry? Mine is enveloping people in encouraging and loving words and, as you can tell from my writing, I love doing it!

I mean what's not to love? I get to work for God Almighty and work my way to heaven and get blessings here at the same time!

Love on Fire
If you can see my enthusiasm and love in the things that I do
Emulate me and let that loving fire become a part of you
And find your place in the work of saving and encouraging souls
As you move toward eternity and your heavenly goal.

I accomplish my ministry of love through speaking and writing encouraging words. Again, what is yours? Don't know yet? Start looking to see what more you can do for God.

Case in Point

I have had people to stand in line at several places where I have spoken to shake my hand. The first time that it happened, I was taken aback. The next time, I was less taken aback and more introspective.

Let me tell you a little about the first time it happened to me about three months back. I had just finished doing a ladies' day at a congregation, and when the program was over, people formed a line and stood there waiting their turn to hug me, shake my hand and offer platitudes! Even little kids came up to me! One little baby came up to me and just squeezed my legs. She just squeezed so hard and held on. She held on long enough that I began to wonder and her grandmother looked at me in amazement.

 You see, Y'all, I am living today by the prayers of my Momma and, too, the prayers that I prayed in the yesterday of my youth when I asked to, "Be somebody one day." (Chopping My Row, p. 81)

One by One

The great ones are leaving
One by one
Would that we will have done as much
When our last days are done.

My Point Is

Some of you have probably thought to yourself, "I don't have a gift." To that, I say, "Hogwash!" Everybody has something that they can excel at. *(1 Peter 4:10-11, KJV)* Find something that you just love, love to do and do it in the name and honor of the Lord God. If you like to cook, do that, if you like to crochet, do that, if you like to manicure lawns, do that, if you like to smile and greet people, do that, etc. (What is it that you love to do and seem to be a natural at?)

Do You Command Attention

Are you one of those people who command attention when you speak? Oh, so you haven't really thought about it. Well, think about it and be aware of folks' reactions when you take part in a conversation. Notice how others respond when you are asked a question.

Do you say things that often elicit laughter or giggles from others? Are you one of those people that others love to be around and they usually tell you so? If you are, you may have a talent or gift for encouraging or making glad.

You have the gift of gab. Well, what are you doing with it? Why don't you jot some of the witty things down or write out your viewpoints on certain things that grab your attention? You have seen that you see into things more deeply than most people. You say, "That's just the way I am. I've always been able to do that."

Good, now use that gift to lighten the burdens of more than your immediate circle. How? Write a witty saying book entitled, "Something to Laugh About," or some other catchy name. *(Who says you can't write a book? You are only limited by your vision of what you can do. Don't you know that with God, all things are possible? (Matthew 19:26) How do I know? Easy, I wrote nine. Yes, nine! Need a bit of help getting started? No problem, send me a message and we will see if we can get you started.)*

So you don't have the gift of gab, but people love your cooking, especially your cakes, huh? Good, now take it to the next level and bake once a week for the local homeless shelter or food kitchen. If you have to go there and cook it, then volunteer there for a quick moment. Share the gift that you have with the rest of the world, especially those outside of your usual circle.

You see, the fact that you have always been able to do a certain thing, whether commanding an audience, writing an encouraging word or baking a good cake, etc. all mean that you have a gift for that particular thing. Whether you were born with it or it came later in life, if folks can benefit from it, use it to serve others and glorify God. *(1 Peter 4:10-11, KJV)*

Finding something you are good at and using it for the good of mankind brings glory to God because He gave you the gift in the first place. I mean think about it. Why did you have to be the one who is good at making people laugh, baking a cake, saying encouraging words, etc.? Why you and not your brother or sister? Exactly, you are meant to use that special gift. *(Ephesians 2:10, KJV)*

Case in Point - A Good Return on Investments

I thought that I would give you a personal testimony of how we can give back to the Lord God. I hope that this lesson blesses you as much as it did me to be able to prepare it for you.

Several weeks ago, I received a correspondence from a lady who had recently lost her mother and about how, as she was going through her mother's things, she came upon a book of my poetry. She told me that the book had been marked on the page where the poem, "Happenstance" was printed. She said that the words of that poem reached out and touched her in a weary place in her soul. Then she thanked me for being the "limb that she was able to grab a hold of."

Here is a copy of the poem:

Happenstance
In any new quandary in which
You happen to have been thrown
Look for similarities to past experiences
That you made it through and
By which you have grown.
You will find that fate, though fickle
Will often toss you a limb
That you can grab a hold off
Depending upon your whim.

In any new circumstance, always
Learn as much as you can
Because you never know when you
May need to draw upon your past
To tackle new jobs head on and
To perform accompanying tasks.
1 Peter 5

In the Bible in **Isaiah 50:4** we find what the Lord has to say about encouraging the weary. I'm giving you two different Bible versions of the same scripture.

Contemporary English Version of the Bible
The LORD God gives me the right words to encourage the weary. Each morning he awakens me eager to learn his teaching;

GOD'S WORD® Translation
The Almighty LORD will teach me what to say so I will know how to encourage weary people. Morning after morning he will wake me to listen like a student.

That is what it is all about for me, being an encourager. And though I was the vessel that penned the poem, it was the glory of God shining through me that helped that young lady, you know? He knew that one day I would need to have written the words to that poem to pick that young lady up, so He had me to do it ahead of time. That is the beauty of the way that the Lord God works. And that is what is so phenomenal about His love for us and why I love Him so much. You see, He showed me before I was born that I am of great value to Him because of the price that He paid for me.

1 Corinthians 6:20 For you have been bought with a price: therefore glorify God in your body.

He made an investment in me and that is why I keep doing what I do. I have to keep on doing what I do for Him because I want to make sure that He gets a good return. If I can make the difference for just one person, then I know that my Father is pleased with the way I use the gift (s) that He gave me.

The First Time

You are usually filled with zeal the first time that you attempt to do something new though you know it may be a challenge. The reason that it is a challenge is the fact that there are so many variables that you have not dealt with before. You take the first time that you try out a new recipe or the first time that you try to learn a new skill such as Tunisian crochet. You rarely get it right the first time. With the recipe you have to do trial and error several times, each time tweaking a certain ingredient. Often it is adding a little extra this, cutting back on a little of that, omitting a certain ingredient or substituting another ingredient. Yet because you want to master the recipe you keep at it until you get it to your satisfaction.

I mentioned Tunisian crochet in the paragraph above. That is one of the easiest pretty forms of crochet, I think. Oh, but let me tell you. It was not as simple for me at first. What with being sure that I was picking up the correct thread on the end, remembering to skip the first bar, etc. I did more pulling out than I wanted to. Yet, I persevered and am having a blast with it right now. Of course, I have to deal with the yarn wanting to curl, tsk, tsk. But I like it enough to keep at it. That is the way it is with something that you really want to do.

Remember the things that I talked about being good at so that the Lord can get the glory? Well, just like you have to practice to become good at doing secular things, you have to practice in order to become proficient at the things that you do for the Lord. My point is, "Do the best that you can for Him because the rewards will be worth it, you know?"

A thought to ponder: *Tunisian crochet makes a really warm blanket to snuggle under during the cold season. Have you ever thought about giving some to residents in the nursing homes that have no family to visit them?*

I have listed several scriptures below that talk about the gifts that we have been given.

Matthew 25:15
And to one he gave five talents, to another, two, and to another, one, each according to his own ability...journey.

1 Timothy 6:20
O Timothy, guard what has been entrusted to you, avoiding worldly and empty chatter and the opposing arguments of what is falsely called "knowledge"- Don't waste the gift that you have been given, but use them for the good of yourself and others.

Lift Up Your Voice

1 Peter 4:10
As each one has received a special gift, employ it in serving one another, as good stewards of the manifold grace of God. Make sure that He is getting a good return on the investment that He made in you.

1 Thessalonians 5:11 ESV
Therefore encourage one another and build one another up, just as you are doing. Be kind.

Hebrews 10:25 ESV
Not neglecting to meet together, as is the habit of some, but encouraging one another, and all the more as you see the Day drawing near. Come together and edify one another with love.

Proverbs 16:24 ESV
Gracious words are like a honeycomb, sweetness to the soul and health to the body.

Proverbs 12:25 ESV
Anxiety in a man's heart weighs him down, but a good word makes him glad.

Our God
How about this God that we serve
He made you and me *(Creator)*
He saved you and me *(Jesus' blood)*
He blessed and keeps on blessing you and me
(gifts to use in service for Him)
He is preparing an everlasting place of abode for you and me
How blessed we are to be able to serve this
Creator of all Humanity!

But That's not Me or I Am not Comfortable Doing That

Sometimes you have to leave the flock to become the soaring eagle that you were meant to be and find the place to which you belong and build your nest upon rocky crags. What is it that you do well? Will you let yourself stand out against the masses to do it for Him? And remember that when the Lord has singled you out, you cease to be like everybody else, so stop fighting it. Let's be willing to shine for the Lord!

We talked about doing a job that sometimes you feel is too big for you. And this morning when I heard the thunder roaring in the predawn hours, the magnitude of His power made me think that I needed to visit the topic of, In service to Him," just a little bit more.

There is nothing that He gives you to do that is too big for you to do because the Voice that roars with such magnitude that it makes the earth tremble and makes all of creation stop and take notice is the Power that is behind you. There is nothing and nobody that can keep you from doing what He wants you to do. Will there be pitfalls and traps set, yes. But all will be to no avail because Heaven is with you and that is that!

You see, you never know, as God's servant where your next field of work will be. This is something that I have learned over the course of my life. And there have been times indeed, that I felt like I was not capable of doing the task that was set before me. But I did as I was taught to do, and that was to pray and give the work my best effort as a preacher's wife. Then I waited for the Lord to do His thing and make the work successful.

Rising to the Task

Different jobs require different amounts of diligence. Some can be done with a modicum of effort and others are very exacting. That is a fact of life.

We work and work at trying to accomplish something and when we do, let us remember to give God the praise and the glory for His patience and help in all things in our lives. The Lord has work just waiting in the plan, so be prepared to bloom wherever you are planted.

As I look back over my life I can see a pattern of learning/training there. Take a look at this poem that I wrote for you this morning to illustrate my point.

Learning to Rise to the Task

There have been some tasks in life that tasked my skill set sore
Each time I had given my best, the task or taskmaster
At hand, seemed to require more.
You take the family that I was born into, for example
Its matriarch, my Mother, brooked no quarter
Her motto was, "There is only one way to do it
And that is to do it right."
So, I quickly learned that when doing a job for her
The only way she would be satisfied was to do
That job, to what I called, "the extreme"
Then and only then, she would be satisfied, it seemed.

So when I went to school and had a teacher
That drove us as hard as she could while
Threatening and spanking us whenever we did not do
All that she thought we should
It was no problem for me to do all that she asked

Because my Momma had schooled me in
The art of performing extreme tasks.

And after I graduated high school and made my way to college
The extreme requirements of the professors did not
Bother me much at all
Because all I had to do was allow the extreme training
That I had endured as a child to kick in
And most of my professor's hearts I could win
And if I could not win their hearts, their grudging
Respect was not long in forthcoming
Because I had been trained by our family's Matriarch
To the tune of anybody's drum to be able to march.

Thus when I got my first job in a public school
The stringent requirements, a lesser person would have deterred
But not me because I kicked myself into overdrive and
Said, "There is only one way to do it and that is to do it right,"
Which to my mind meant taking it to the "nth" degree
Because that is the way that my training at
My Momma's hands had prepared me.

As I moved on in life and bosses came and went
Each subsequent boss would say, "I have heard about you
What a good job you do and all, but each person here
Will be judged on what you do for me and not on what I hear
So, if you do your job, you will have nothing to fear
But if you slack, sooner or later, I will be asking you to let
The front door hit your back.

After I retired from teaching and worked in the compacity
Of a grant compliance person as a housing coordinator
All of my life's training stood me in good stead
Because I had learned to dot every "i" and cross every "t"

Lift Up Your Voice

For if anyone was going to be caught half-stepping
That person was not going to be me.

Yes, life has taught me to do things to the "nth" degree
The extent of that "nth" depending upon the place
Where my current life assignment happened to be.

So, when I ended up being married to a preacher
And having to live my life under a microscope
I stood the scrutiny without much of a qualm
Why? I had been taught to, "rise to the task"
Because of the Matriarch that I was given as a teacher.

Now, each day is pretty much a delight as I think
About the Beneficent Hands that placed me in a family
Where I could receive my foundational training
For the road that had been laid out for me.
So, if you have a job in life that is proving to be taxing for you,
Give it all you have because it may be a practice round
For the next job that you will be given to do.

A Task Too Big for You
There are times that you are given tasks
That you feel are too big for you
You feel that you are just not equipped
To do the task that you have been asked to do.

If the job fell your lot to do,
Then the job was meant for you.
Always look at difficult tasks
As training for a bigger one.

And too, think about the faith that
He must have in you to give you
Such a difficult job to do.
He might be saying,
"You are stronger than you think you are,
And I'll show you."

So, what you must do is attempt the task
And often you will find that through the
Process of trial and error, you will get it done
With enough completeness that you can
See that you were the correct one
To do the task that you were given
And you bask in the seeds of joyous completion
Forgetting about the weeds of doubt
By which you were often driven.

What a joy it is to be loved and guided by a Father
Who looks past any trials, traps, and pitfalls
That happen to be in our road
And lifts you up enough so that you do not
Fail under the pressure of such a heavy load.

So look upon each hard task as training
Against the day that in your daily life
It will be raining.

"Job well done," is coming up
And the loving Savior's smile that goes with it
And your face with its answering smile
With triumph, will be lit.

No Task Too Difficult or Hard
Keep your head up and your hand to the plow
And keep working your assigned row with the
Cockleburs, morning glories, Johnson grass and all
Because the God of Heaven will not let you fall.
Step on from this day forward with a renewed zeal
And you will see that your parents' God is still real.

You see, I thought that I could not work as hard
As I used to for the Lord because the death of
My Momma and my brothers had me feeling lost and alone.
But now, I have a healthier respect for that verse
In Philippians 4:13 that reads, "I can do all things through
Christ Who strengthens me" as I continue to keep stepping on.

I have learned to submerge myself in the love
Of Jehovah Tsori/Jehovah Rophe, Who
Looks down upon me from Heaven above.

Mission Accomplished
There are times when it seems that we
Are handed Herculean tasks to get done
And because of the direness of the situation
It seems that there is nothing to do but put
Your shoulder to the grindstone and give it a go
But oh the unmitigated joy you will feel when
You finish said task, don't you know?
Often in accomplishing such tasks, you have
To push this, pull that, tweak a little here, cajole there, etc.
But the end result is a Herculean task that's
Been whittled down to size
With you standing beaming with winner's pride
And giving thanks to God, Who never left your side.

See What the Lord Has Done!

For Allowing Me to See

People come to me for encouragement and advice
And always have done
But I couldn't see the magnitude of the gift in me
Until I was approached by my only son.

Thank You, Lord, for allowing me to see
The gift that you have placed in me
And for allowing me to use it for all folks,
Including self and family.

I am grateful, honored, and humbled all at the same time.

Shining My Light

Whatever I do today, Lord
I want to bring glory to You
Be it working within my home
Visiting the sick, or greeting a stranger
I want to let You shine forth
In all that I do.

Just a Little Nobody

I am just a little nobody
Who hails from Tennessee
Who believed my Momma
And my Bible school teacher
And my secular teacher three
When they told me that I could
Be whatever I wanted to be.

So don't be surprised when

Lift Up Your Voice

You see me going on, in spite of
And being all that I can be while
Doing all that I can for Him
Because I have a goal that I am trying to reach
And that is to make it to my prepared place
In the beautiful city above
That is full of joy and love.

****

He kept me
So, I'll keep keeping on
He never left me
So that, by example
I could show strength
To my fellowmen and
Say without words, "I am not alone."
I am supported by the Power
Of Heaven's Throne.

****

Moses had a rod that the
Lord turned into a snake
David had a sling that the
Fall of Goliath did bring
For God can use most anything
That you have in your possession
To gain sinners' attention and
Bring them to repentance and confession.

If there is something that you like to do a lot
Then practice doing it for the Lord
And see what winds up shimmering in your pot

You may have a captive audience waiting
Whether you realize it or not.

****

Many things happen in life that I don't understand
Sometimes I wonder what drives me and
Makes me so different from my fellowman
It is then that I remember that I am not my own
But that I was created for a purpose by the
God Who sits on Heaven's throne
It is then that I remember that I am
What God made me
Even though this world, my worth, may not see
I am what the Lord God meant me to be
Within myself, I am just Alma
Me.

****

If Ever
If you ever find yourself wondering why you
Keep going when most folk would have quit
Why you keep going through sheer determination
Just know that you are what God made you to be
Perhaps an example for some others to see
Then too, your rough times may be
Stepping stones to a greater destiny.

Recap

What better thing to do than use the gift that you take for granted
for the glory of the God Who gave it to you? Hmm-m-m?

Command attention through service and give God the glory. Be blessed and bless somebody else by passing the blessing forward. I just did.

Thus, you have my take on saying and doing a bit more for God.

Discussion Questions

1. According to Luke 10:27, what should be our demeanor as we work for the Lord?

_____

_____

_____

_____

2. Do all of us have things that we excel at?

_____

_____

_____

_____

3. According to Ephesians 2:10, why are we given certain things that we excel at?

_____

_____

_____

_____

4. Who gets the glory when we excel at tasks that we have undertaken in our Christian duty?

_____

_____

_____

_____

What Do You Think

1. Should the preacher's wife or leaders's wives be the only ones willing to take on uncomfortable tasks? Why?

_____

_____

_____

_____

For Further Reading
1 Corinthians 12:5-6; Romans 12:6-8, 35; Matthew 22:37-39; Hebrews 10:25; Matthew 25:15; 1 Timothy 6:20; 1 Samuel 10:24; Psalm 139:13-16

Roses on a Cold Day
Well, the kids are grown and gone
The husband is off on a twelve-hour round trip
Our latest and the last of the family pets has
Long since been laid to rest
And there is just me for right now in the family nest
Yep, I am at home alone.
I can smell my chili simmering in the pot
And since I will dine alone this afternoon, I can have
It whenever I want to, with cornbread, saltine crackers or not.
There are a myriad of chores that I could do
But this cold February Saturday morning this woman
Is going to curl up with a good book beside the fire
With a warm cup of tea and travel with one
Of my favorite authors to a port across the sea.
Late tonight or early in the a.m.
I will be a preacher's wife again with
The hustle and bustle that goes along with the job
But this cold Saturday morning, I'm just
Going to read, rest, nap, crochet and

Have a day of forced but contented quiet
As I sit beside the glowing log with its dancing fire
And twiddle my toes in leisure because there
Is nothing from me, at this moment, that people require
Since I've done my writing for the day
And said what I needed to say.

About the Author

Alma L. Carr-Jones, a beloved educator, poet/author, a retired educator and a motivational speaker, lives in McKenzie, TN. She is a successful author of nine books to date. Alma loves to write because, as she is fond of saying, "It is something I was meant to do."

She is:

- An Avid Inspirational Daily Blog Writer www.almacarr-jones.blogspot.com
- A Highly Acclaimed Retired Teacher of 30 Years
- Author of Nine Books
- A Preacher's Wife of 40 years
- A w.o.w. (woman of work for the MASTER's use)

This Christian lady is one who really tries to live up to her motto of "Doing What I Can, While I Can." Since she is quite busy doing whatever her hands find to do, that old saying of *wearing out instead of rusting out* will be true of her. She says she wants to have made a difference in the lives of her fellowmen and to have built a legacy that will still speak, even after she is planted in the ground.

To have the treasure of this woman's work in your home is to have a loving dose of life as viewed from the eyes of a preacher's daughter's daughter and the wife of a preacher. This woman has a heart of gold with arms big enough and ears tender enough to help any soul stay encouraged as they make their way toward Heaven. Alma is such a jewel of a woman that she says, when you see her doing something that you admire, "Don't get it twisted; it is not me, but the glory of GOD shining through me."

Other Books by the Author

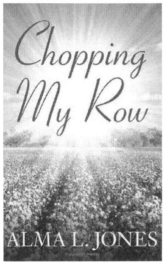 

Available on Amazon and from the Author

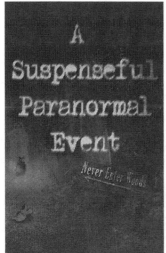
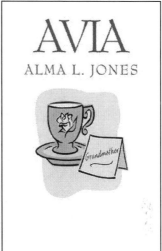

And More of
The Tallest Mountain Series

Available Now in Paperback and on Kindle
Purchase on Amazon and from most booksellers by request

Coming Soon:

Thank you
for reading our books!

Look for other books
published by

www.TMPbooks.com

www.TMPbooks.com

*If you enjoyed this book
please remember to leave a review!*

Made in the USA
Columbia, SC
21 July 2021

42128610R00091